TACTIC **FOR**
CHANGING
YOUR LIFE

G000122785

TACTICS
FOR CHANGING YOUR LIFE

ANTONY KIDMAN

KOGAN
PAGE

First published in Australia in 1986 by
Biochemical & General Services, PO Box 156,
St Leonards, NSW, Australia 2065;
reprinted 1987, 1988.

This edition first published in Great Britain
in 1989 by Kogan Page Limited,
120 Pentonville Road, London N1 9JN.

British Library Cataloguing in Publication Data

Kidman, Antony D.
    Tactics for changing your life: a self -
    help manual
    1. Self - Development
    I. Title
    158'.1

    ISBN 1-85091-939-9
    ISBN 1-85091-940-2 Pbk

Typeset by DP Photosetting, Aylesbury, Bucks
Printed and bound in Great Britain by
Biddles Ltd, Guildford

Contents

Acknowledgements

I would like to thank Dr Albert Ellis and Dr Susan Presby of the Institute for Rational-Emotive Therapy in New York for their supervision of individual therapy sessions and advice.

I wish to thank the following for permission to reproduce copyright material:

Dr Aaron T Beck for the Beck depression inventory on pages 34–35 (© 1978 Aaron T Beck, MD); the cognition checklist and the counting statements on pages 90–91 (© 1977 Aaron T Beck, MD); the Daily Record of Dysfunctional Thoughts Form appearing on pages 30–33 (© 1977 Aaron T Beck, MD).

Further information about the Beck depression inventory and the dysfunctional thoughts schedule and/or permission to use and reproduce these may be obtained from the Center for Cognitive Therapy, Room 602, 133 South 36th Street, Philadelphia, Pennsylvania 19104. The cognition checklist and the counting statements are taken from the treatment manual *Cognitive Therapy of Substance Abuse* by Aaron T Beck, MD and Gary Emery, PhD.

The Institute for Rational-Emotive Therapy, New York, to reproduce the diagram on page 19 and the RET Self-Help Form on pages 106–109.

Professor Peter M Lewinsohn of the Department of Psychology of the University of Oregon to use parts of his book *Control Your Depression*, in particular, the pleasant events schedule shown on pages 43–51.

Dr R W Novaco of the University of California, Irvine, to use parts of his anger inventory from his book *Program in Social Ecology* on pages 71–73.

The *Business Review Weekly* to reproduce parts of articles by Antony Kidman from the editions of 6 October 1984; 3 November 1984; 1 February 1985; and 6 September 1985.

I would like to thank Janelle Kidman for her editorial comments and corrections.

Preface

The topics which appear in this manual have arisen from my interest in stress management but mainly as a result of my exposure to the writings of Dr Albert Ellis, founder of rational-emotive therapy and director of the Institute for Rational-Emotive Therapy in New York.

It was his writings, together with my training at the Institute for Rational-Emotive Therapy, that enabled me to formulate many of the ideas expressed here.

I would also like to acknowledge the concepts of depression that have been proposed by Professor Tim Beck of the University of Pennsylvania where I was fortunate to spend a short time at his Center for Cognitive Therapy.

Professor Arnold Lazarus's writings, especially on multi-modal therapy, have also been very helpful.

My own work with clients and groups in trying to help them manage depression and related problems generated much information and I have used several case histories as examples.

My scientific background has taught me to be as objective as possible, but psychotherapy, and in particular rational-emotive therapy, has given me a greater understanding of myself and human behaviour in general that studies in chemistry, biochemistry and neuropharmocology could not.

My research into human behaviour gives me hope that humans as conscious, thinking and reflective beings can do much by learning and hard work to overcome the self-disturbance that plagues us all from time to time.

Antony Kidman

CHAPTER 1
How to Use This Manual

Introduction

Tactics for Changing Your Life is a self-help manual for people who want to change aspects of their behaviour which they do not like. Almost all human beings appear to have either learned or innate tendencies to behave in a self-defeating way at times. Some of us get bitterly hostile about small slights or the trivial actions of others, such as someone tooting his horn at a red light, or a shop assistant not serving you quickly enough. Others feel intensely guilty over things they have done in the past, or what they think they should have done, such as spent time with difficult children.

Many of us start to blame ourselves, the boss, our parents, our teachers, for our perceived shortcomings and lack of success. These tendencies and the consequent negative feelings which occur frequently reduce our chances of achieving goals and enjoying life. This manual is designed to show you techniques you can use to change your undesirable behaviour which depends on your feelings and which in turn depends on your thinking. It may be that you want to change your reactions to others, to be more friendly, to reduce your anger and hostility, to stop smoking or drinking, or to improve your relationship with your spouse, children or workmates. Improvements in these areas will mean an increased chance of obtaining your goals and enjoying your existence.

There is no magic in this approach, it is based on research evidence and analysis by many intelligent behavioural psychologists. You may find that none of these techniques suits you, but at least give them a try.

Many undesirable behaviour patterns appear to be learnt during childhood. Our genes may react poorly with the environment which may be another source of self-defeating tendencies. This does not mean that you cannot change, rather that generally only by working hard and persistently can you unlearn thinking and behaviour that has been with you for years; only by stubbornly refusing to give in can you overcome, say, a biological predisposition to over-react aggressively to a verbal insult. The evidence is by no means clear why people behave the way they do, but it is in their interests to try to change for the reasons I have outlined above.

When people work at changing themselves there are frequent relapses and progress is often two steps forward, one step back. Do not give up until you have given it a good try, and even if you fail at a particular activity, say to stop smoking, you as a human being are not a failure.

Another advantage of mastering these techniques and learning how to challenge your irrational thinking is that you will be much better equipped to deal with the inevitable frustrations and irritations of normal living. People who are seeking a perfect harmonious world, free of disturbance, unhappiness and pain will almost invariably be disappointed because loved ones die, teeth have to be extracted occasionally, injuries and sickness occur and, ultimately, we must die. Thus, if you can develop resources and techniques to alter your attitude to these problems, you are in a much better position to deal with and to manage them in the future.

Using the manual

I suggest that you read the chapter entitled Tactics For Change first and then select the topics that interest you most. The chapters, as far as possible, stand on their own and can be read as such, and for this reason certain principles, phrases and references are repeated in several chapters. Chapters 6 to 9, Fear of Failing, Hostility at Work, Personal Organisation and Coping With Change, were written for people in the workplace; however, the techniques are applicable in any setting.

The self-assessment forms are intended to assist you to obtain information about yourself; they include the Beck depression inventory (pages 34–37) and the Novaco anger inventory (pages 71–73). They are not infallible and are only intended to give you an indication of how you perceive yourself at the time you fill them in.

The Daily Record of Dysfunctional Thoughts Form (pages 30–37) and the RET Self-Help Form (pages 106–109) are tools intended to assist you to use the techniques described in Chapters 2 and 3. They are used to dispute and manage irrational thoughts and self-defeating behaviour.

The time management forms at the end of Chapter 8 can be used for setting goals and scheduling activities on a regular basis.

References for further reading are listed. They will allow you to pursue a particular subject in more detail.

Do not be afraid to share your feelings and thoughts with trusted friends, even though you may be anxious about doing so. Do not be afraid to seek professional help either, as it is not shameful to get therapeutic advice when the need arises; it may well lead to a different perception of yourself and your environment and a more adaptive response to it.

References

A Ellis, *Reason and Emotion in Psychotherapy*, Citadel, USA (1985)

J D Frank, *Persuasion and Healing*, Schocken, New York (1963)

V E Frankl, *Man's Search for Meaning*, 2nd edition, Hodder & Stoughton (1987)

CHAPTER 2
Tactics for Change

How many times have you heard a friend, a relative, a spouse say, 'Well, that's the way I am, take me or leave me! I've always been like this and I always will be!' I imagine that you have heard those words many times, probably with a certain amount of disquiet. However, it is a common belief and people are quite willing to attribute their behaviour to their genes, their parents' treatment of them, their spouse, their work and so on and believe they cannot change. Yet thousands of people are changing their undesirable behaviour patterns, often talking to therapists, reading books, attending lectures or going to special group meetings.

How do I stop smoking? How do I stop drinking? How do I stop over-eating? How can I become less anxious about my boss/my children/my spouse? What can I do about my temper? 'I have a very short fuse and I seem to be getting more and more angry with people and things in general.' Other problems that people have are fears of being killed in an aeroplane or unbearable panic on leaving the house. Recently a senior executive told me, 'I have to speak in public and sometimes I am so fearful of getting up in front of a group of people that I am sick at the very thought of it.'

I believe there is not one of us who would not want to change some aspect of our behaviour in order to enjoy life more and get on better with people both at work and at home. Yet we don't seem to be able to do it; we keep doing things that cause us and others distress and hurt.

Unfortunately, this is the way human beings are; they have a great propensity to generate anxiety, hostility and depression in themselves because of what they perceive going on around them.

As humans, we often make mistakes and do irrational things. We expect a great deal of ourselves and others and when we fail, we devalue and condemn each other. We demand that the world gives us a good living, that others be fair and just, that our spouses be interested in all that we do and that our children and colleagues behave as we expect and as we feel they *should* behave. These expectations of ourselves and others will frequently lead to self-disturbance.

Requirements for change

Millions of people around the world have changed their lives in ways that they want. They enjoy life more by doing so and they survive better as human beings. Generally the following are necessary:

- a desire to change;
- the belief that it is possible to change;
- usually some interaction with others, perhaps a professional in the mental health field or by joining a special group; sometimes by talking to a friend or even reading a particular book to learn suitable techniques;
- a plan for change together with steps which can be taken to achieve it;
- effective monitoring of change which occurs usually in increments with rewards for successful progress.

Techniques

Sigmund Freud, the founder of modern psychotherapy, attempted to change the undesirable behaviour patterns in his clients by probing their subconscious, using free association, getting them to work through their difficulties. This helped some people. With the development of his ideas and publication of his books, many new techniques were developed to assist people in dealing with their problems. Since then, hundreds of theories and schools of psychotherapy have appeared which have had varying degrees of success and there is still much controversy over the efficacy of some of them.

I would like to share some of the ideas from the cognitive behavioural school of psychotherapy which I have used in my own work. This cognitive behavioural approach stems from the premise that people's perceptions or belief systems determine their response to events going on around them and that these responses generate their feelings and consequent behaviour. Thus the response of a man to being told that his girlfriend, with whom he is very much in love, is about to leave him varies enormously. Some men would react with extreme hostility and anger, others would feel depressed and perhaps even suicidal, while others might feel appropriately disappointed or annoyed, even sad, but nevertheless would do all they could to change the situation and yet accept that perhaps she would leave anyway and that life goes on. This last group, with their rational response, would not berate themselves or be utterly depressed for weeks or months on end, but continue with their daily lives, making plans about the future, perhaps seeking a new relationship and generally coping fairly well.

These individuals are telling themselves different things about the same event and it is the thinking that is different, eg some are saying, 'She should not leave me because I am charming, upright, dependable and altogether a marvellous person', others are saying, 'I am boring, dull and a worthless person, no wonder she left', whereas more appropriate thinking would be, 'It would be much better if she did not leave, and I would prefer that she did not, but unfortunately this can happen, perhaps I'd better look at some of the reasons for her leaving, either to salvage the situation or to prevent a recurrence should I establish a new relationship.'

Rational-Emotive Therapy

Ellis calls his form of psychotherapy Rational-Emotive Therapy and uses a simple ABC system to explain it. A is the activating event – spouse or girlfriend says she is leaving. This leads to C, feelings and behaviour, eg being upset, angry or depressed. However, you will notice that B has been left out: this is the belief system – 'She shouldn't do this to me, I am a very important person.' Ellis and his colleagues would argue in order to change this man's negative emotions and consequent behaviour, he must change his irrational thinking – in this case, dissuade himself from blaming his girlfriend, getting angry, getting depressed, thinking of suicide or whatever thoughts are going on in his mind to produce the self-defeating behaviour. If he continues with the irrational belief system, his effectiveness at work and with other people who depend on him will be undermined. Furthermore, thinking about his depression or anger, makes him worse. A critical technique to produce change is to stand back from a situation, observe yourself and dispute in your own mind the thinking which is going to lead to the actions which you know will worsen and defeat you. (See diagram of Rational-Emotive Therapy's ABC theory of emotional disturbance overleaf.)

Cognitive behavioural therapy draws on a whole range of techniques to help people overcome their undesirable actions. People can then reward themselves when they overcome an addiction such as over-eating. When they have reached a weight loss by their target date they will treat themselves to a film they have been wanting to see or by calling someone they like very much, or some other enjoyable activity. Alternatively, if they over-eat and don't keep to their diet on a particular day, they can discipline themselves by calling someone they don't like or by doing some unpleasant task. This behaviour therapy approach stresses the importance of recording in a diary events which have occurred and changes you are introducing, so that you can study and check your progress.

Common irrational ideas

I would like to mention a number of common irrational ideas that we frequently have which lead to negative feelings and emotions.

- *The dire need for success and approval*

    Karen Horney, a famous psychoanalyst, noted a few years ago that most of us run our lives by the *'tyranny of the shoulds'* and the worst 'should' of the lot is probably as follows: 'I should

A
Activating experience

Woman friend breaks the news that she is going out with another man, and therefore wishes to break off the relationship with you.

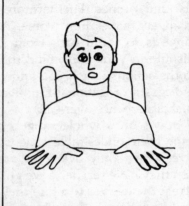

B
Belief about (or interpretation of) the experience

'I really must be a worthless person.'

'I'll *never* find another great woman like her.'

'*She* doesn't want me; therefore *no* one could possibly want me.'

and/or

'This is *awful!*'   'Everything happens to me!'

'That bitch! She *shouldn't be that way.*'

'*I can't stand* the world being so unfair and lousy.'

Rational-Emotive Therapy's ABC theory of emotional disturbance

'Men are disturbed not by things, but by the view which they take of them.'

Epictetus, first century AD

It is not the event, but rather it is our interpretation of it, that causes our emotional reaction.

C

upsetting emotional Consequences

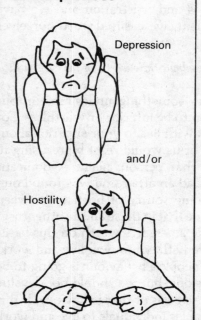

Depression

and/or

Hostility

D

Disputing of irrational ideas

'Where's the evidence that because this woman wishes to end our relationship, that I am a worthless person; or that I'll *never* be able to have a really good relationship with someone else; or even that I couldn't be happy alone?'

and/or

'Why is it *awful* that I'm not getting what I want?'

'Why *shouldn't* the world be full of injustices?'

E

new Emotional consequence or Effect

Sadness: 'Well, we did have a nice relationship, and I'm sorry to see it end – but it did have its problems and now I can go out and find a new friend.'

or

Annoyance: 'It's annoying that she was seeing someone but it isn't awful or intolerable.'

19

succeed perfectly at the goals I select and value and win utter and unreserved approval from everyone I consider to be significant to my achievements.' With this 'should' laid upon our shoulders, we frequently make ourselves feel anxious, depressed, despairing, insecure and inadequate. Even when there is relatively little stress and frustration and we have unusual competence and talent, we easily disturb ourselves with this assumption.

- *The propensity to rate people and evaluate their worth on the basis of their behaviour*
  Because an individual does something undesirable in our eyes, we consider that person to be inferior or worthless. For example, someone you work with lies to your superior about you and you find out. Most of us would react by refusing to have anything to do with that person again. A domestic example would be if a man had an affair and was found out, then it could be a never-ending source of hostility between him and his wife. I would argue that in these and all other cases as soon as you start to decide a person's worth on this basis, you will devalue many people with whom you live and work.
  The principle here is that people's behaviour is going to be disappointing on many occasions, but we should not devalue or denigrate the person on the basis of that behaviour. If this principle is understood, it enables individuals to live and work with other people more easily and to resolve conflicts. That does not mean that you have to *like* the person who has upset you or spend your free time with people whose behaviour you dislike. However, in a job situation or even at home, it means that you can cooperate with them when it is necessary and in your interest to do so.

- *The dire need for fair treatment and justice*
  This irrational idea takes the following form: 'People *must* treat me kindly, considerately and fairly at all times and when they don't they are terrible individuals who deserve blame and punishment.' With this Utopian idea, we easily make ourselves angry, resentful, vindictive and depressed. Human beings, being fallible and vulnerable, are most unlikely to act in the

kindly and ethical way we would wish at all times.

- *The dire need for immediate and constant gratification of needs*

   Many people believe that the conditions under which they live must make things easy for them. The world should give them practically all they want and they must be prevented from undergoing severe deprivations, pain or stress. If one believes this, it is very easy to acquire intense feelings of self-pity and anger.

- *If something is, or may be, dangerous or frightening, you should be terribly concerned about the possibility of it happening*

   This is an irrational belief because, although it is often wise to think in advance about dangers and pitfalls and plan to avert them, what you normally feel as anxiety or intense fear is rarely helpful and generally lessens your ability to prevent or deal with any real danger. Let us say you are walking down a dark street and three tough-looking characters approach from the other end. If you start telling yourself that this is an extremely dangerous situation, 'I could be attacked or injured,' and similar thoughts without assessing the situation more calmly, you may, by running and screaming or appearing terrified, let would-be assailants know that you are fearful and therefore a perfect target for a robbery, assault or whatever. They may have had nothing in mind, meanwhile you have given yourself a tremendous amount of anxiety which may affect you for several hours, whereas if you had remained alert and were able to assess the situation clearly, then you would have been able to take steps to cross to the other side of the road in a controlled, positive manner or planned to enter a house as though it were one you were familiar with and knew people inside, or some other course of action that would have reduced the chance of an attack.

Worrying intensely about the possibility of some dire events will *not prevent* them from occurring; it may even contribute to bringing them about. Anxiety about having a car accident may make you so nervous that you then drive into another car or post whereas if you were calmer you might easily have avoided this kind of accident.

Some dreaded events, such as becoming seriously ill or dying, are inevitable and nothing, including your worrying about them, can possibly prevent them from occurring. By worrying about those events which you cannot change you create for yourself the additional and often much more crippling disadvantage of being upset long before they actually occur. Thus, if you have a good reason to believe that you will actually die, say from cancer, your worry about this will not only fail to stop it but it will make a misery of your remaining days for you and your family which could perhaps otherwise be peaceful and even happy if you accept the inevitability of your death.

A list of common irrational ideas obtained from Albert Ellis's book *Reason and Emotion in Psychotherapy* is shown on page 23. These irrational tendencies or beliefs can be summarised as the demand and insistence we human beings have for the world to be a perfect place full of perfect people.

Implementing change

The key to implementing change is to think about your thinking. With practice, this can come readily and help you to wind down the inappropriate extremes of negative emotions to more appropriate ones. This does not mean that you are trying to destroy feelings and emotion, quite the reverse. The cognitive behavioural school would argue that positive feelings, such as happiness, joy and ecstasy, can all be increased and enhanced by using these ideas. So unless you enjoy being depressed, bitterly hostile, over-anxious, it is worth learning these techniques to change your thinking. Be on your guard against the 'tyranny of the shoulds or musts'.

The other methods I have mentioned which come from behaviour therapy include careful monitoring and writing down of your activities with agreed rewards and penalties. Talking with professionals, friends, your spouse or participating in a therapy group can help to monitor and reinforce change. The possibilities are great and we all either know or have read of people who have undergone profound changes for the better in their lives. With the availability of these techniques, we can implement change in our own lives – not with ease, because there is generally *no gain without pain*, but it can be done. I hope you will use the techniques described in this book to help bring about changes you want to make in your life.

A special *RET* Self-help Form is shown on pages 106–109 for you to write down and dispute your irrational beliefs.

Common irrational ideas

1. I must be loved or approved of by every significant person in my life.
2. I must be competent, adequate and achieving in all respects if I am to consider myself worthwhile.
3. When people act unfairly or badly, I blame them and they should be severely punished.
4. It is terrible and catastrophic when things are not the way I would very much like them to be.
5. Human unhappiness is caused by external events and people have little or no ability to control their sorrows and disturbances.
6. I must feel anxious if something is or may be dangerous or fearsome and keep dwelling on the possibility of its occurrence.
7. It is easier to avoid than to face certain difficulties in life with responsibility.
8. Everyone should be dependent upon others and I need someone stronger than myself on whom I can rely.
9. I should become quite upset over other people's problems and disturbances.
10. The world should provide me with what I need and when it doesn't, it's a terrible place and I can't stand it.

References

A T Beck, *Cognitive Therapy and Emotional Disorders*, International Universities Press, New York (1976)

A Ellis and R A Harper, *A New Guide to Rational Living*, Wilshire, North Hollywood, California, USA (1975)

A Ellis, *Reason and Emotion in Psychotherapy*, Citadel, USA (1985)

A Lazarus, *The Practice of Multimodal Therapy*, McGraw-Hill, (1981)

CHAPTER 3
Coping With Depression

Recently a woman came into my clinic and said she had no confidence whatsoever in herself, she no longer found any enjoyment in what she did – cooking, her family, her garden, her part-time job – and she could see no escape in sight from this living death that she called existence. She occasionally had thoughts of killing herself but was too afraid to do anything about it. 'I wake up two to three hours early every morning and cannot go back to sleep. I have been feeling like this for six weeks and before that, on and off for weeks at a time for the last ten years, but this is the worst bout of depression I've ever had.' She joined our 'Coping With Depression' group and is now doing much better.

Severe depression affects many thousands of people and about 15 per cent of the population will suffer from it badly enough to warrant professional help. Most will not get it, while the majority of those who do are prescribed tranquillisers or antidepressant drugs and get a few minutes chat from their GP, if they are lucky.

By severe depression I mean something quite distinct from normal sadness and grieving, which is also commonly called 'depression' and something which we all experience as a result of the stresses of normal living, among which are death of a loved one, losing your job, retirement, illness and loss of abilities with age. Clinical, severe depression is profoundly disturbing. It interferes with people's lives to such an extent that they cannot work properly, their relationships are seriously affected and they themselves feel terrible. Only people who have experienced this know how bad it really is.

Many famous people have suffered from depression, including

Charles Darwin, Winston Churchill, Napoleon, Virginia Woolf, Abraham Lincoln, Ernest Hemingway and Vivien Leigh. What can be done to help people who suffer from depression?

Dr A T Beck's clinic at the University of Pennsylvania has developed what he calls cognitive therapy which has been shown to help many moderately to severely depressed individuals. Those who suffer from depression only, as opposed to manic depression, appear to be helped the most, although I believe all can benefit to some extent. I am not suggesting that antidepressant drugs are not beneficial, they most certainly are, it is just that many people experience undesirable side effects and there is no guarantee that the depression will not recur. Treatment with lithium carbonate, discovered by the Australian Dr John Cade in 1949, has yielded excellent results in people suffering from manic depression. However, the problem of side-effects and long-term toxicity makes many people unhappy with medication.

The cognitive triad

Dr Beck and Dr Albert Ellis have shown that they can produce significant improvements in thinking and behaviour by getting depressed people to recognise their negative spontaneous thoughts and to deal with these thoughts.

Dr Beck argues that depressed individuals typically have three opinions that persist:

- a negative view of themselves
- a negative view of the world
- a negative view of the future.

Objective analysis of their lives rarely supports these beliefs, although there may be *some* truth in one or two of them. However, they believe them deeply and completely.

The techniques I am about to describe are aimed at getting depressed people to correct these perceptions and to substitute more realistic thoughts.

Whenever you are feeling down because of a chance remark from an acquaintance, spouse or member of the family, when some minor incident occurs which makes you feel quite unneccessarily sad, or when the recollection of past events triggers unpleasant thoughts and feelings, then you have allowed incorrect thinking to generate depressed feelings.

Typical thinking errors

- *Exaggeration*

    A person who is concerned about health may notice some intestinal aches and pains and immediately conclude that it is stomach cancer; thus some ordinary occurrence, typical of everyday life, becomes an overwhelming disaster. The depressed person not only exaggerates a situation, but also the possible harm which may come from it.

- *Overgeneralising*

    A depressed person may pass a stranger in the street who is frowning. The depressed person believes the frown is specifically directed by the stranger to himself/herself and thinks erroneously, 'Nobody likes me, I am a complete failure.'

- *Ignoring the positive*

    When a depressed woman I was counselling was advised to keep a diary, she realised that *positive* events occurred frequently during her day but that she had a tendency not to pay attention to them. She had ignored the fact that she was a teacher and interacting with her students regularly, imparting useful knowledge to them, and performing an important job. She had also undervalued the advice, guidance and assistance she gave to her own children, as well as the management of the house, the family finances, holidays, shopping and meals.

Depression sufferers need to list their goals and priorities. This technique is described very effectively in Alan Lakein's book *How to Get Control of Your Time and Your Life*. Having done this, they can then decide what steps can be taken to move towards those goals. Perfectionism, in the form of a spotless house, perfect children and the need for approval from family, relatives, friends, and

The ABC of changing feelings

B. Thoughts

You interpret the events with a series of thoughts that continually flow through your mind. This is called your 'self talk'

A. Environment

A series of positive, neutral and negative events

C. Mood

Your feelings are created by your thoughts. All experiences must be processed through your brain and given a conscious meaning before you experience an emotional response

neighbours, can drive a woman into depression. These demands to be perfect are self-defeating because they are impossible to achieve.

Specific steps to help

- *The daily schedule*
  Make a list of items you plan to do each day, assign priorities to them, then keep a record of your actual activities for the day. This can also be done on a weekly, monthly or even a yearly basis, using appropriate plan sheets.

- *The A B C of changing feelings*
  This has been developed by the founder of rational emotive therapy, Dr Albert Ellis.

  Most depressed people believe that their lives are so bad that it is natural for them to feel sad. However, cognitive behavioural theory proposes that your feelings are derived from your belief system or your way of thinking.

  Carefully consider a recent event which has depressed or upset you, divide the incident into three parts, A: the event, B: your thoughts, and C: the consequent feelings and behaviour. Most people are only aware of the event and their feelings. For example, A: your husband forgets your wedding anniversary, C: you feel hurt, sad and disappointed, B: what is really making you unhappy is the meaning you attach to the event. You think: 'My husband's forgetfulness means he doesn't love me any more!' You may then think that without his approval and admiration, you can never be happy or satisfied. However, it is quite possible that your husband was just busy or that he doesn't share your enthusiasm for making a big thing of anniversaries. You have been suffering because of your unwarranted conclusion, not because of the event itself.

- *Disputing negative thoughts*
  Try to correct your negative thoughts by answering each of the negative statements you have made with a positive balanced statement. Another woman participating in our Coping With Depression programme, mentioned that she felt

guilty and depressed because she had received a phone call from a woman friend whose husband had died several months ago. She realised that she had not contacted her friend since his death and feelings of guilt and depression were aroused. She then balanced this negative, automatic thinking with a positive statement to the effect that she had been very busy and her friend would not have rung her anyway if she had not wished the friendship to continue.

These negative thoughts and feelings can be written down, with the balancing, positive statement written alongside. This in itself often helps people to change their feeling of depression into one of appropriate sadness or disappointment.

The final point I would like to make is that there are generally many more options for resolving a situation than we are aware of. Depressed people typically think in black and white terms. Analysis of a problem, either by putting the facts down in writing or discussing it with a good friend, reveals other options and perhaps the realisation that the consequences may not be so terrible. What Albert Ellis calls 'catastrophising' is highly unlikely to occur.

The cognitive approach can be summed up with a quote from the philosopher, Epictetus: 'People are disturbed not by things, but by the view which they take of them.'

On pages 30–31 is a completed Daily Record of Dysfunctional Thoughts Form devised by Professor Tim Beck showing how a depressed person has used the form over several days, plus a blank form that you might like to use yourself.

On pages 34–37 is Professor Beck's inventory which can be filled in over a period of weeks to determine the extent of your depressed state.

Daily Record of Dysfunctional Thoughts

Date	*Situation* Describe: 1. Actual event leading to unpleasant emotion, or 2. Stream of thoughts, daydream, or recollection, leading to unpleasant emotion.	**Emotions(s)** 1. Specify sad; anxious; angry; etc. 2. Rate degree of emotion, 1–100 per cent.	**Automatic thought(s)** 1. Write automatic thought(s) that precede emotion(s) 2. Rate belief in automatic thought(s), 0–100 per cent.
9/8	Received a letter from a friend who was recently married.	Guilty 60%	'I should have gone to her wedding.'
9/9	Was thinking about all the things I wanted to get done over the weekend.	Anxious 40%	'I'll never get all of this done.' 'It's too much for me.'
9/11	Made a mistake ordering supplies.	Anxious 60%	'Pictured my boss yelling at me.'
9/12	Pictured myself being depressed forever.	Depressed 80%	'I'll never get better.'
9/15	My boyfriend called and said he couldn't go out with me.	Depressed 90%	'He doesn't like me *No one* could *ever* like me.'

How to fill in the form

When you experience an unpleasant emotion, note the situation that seemed to stimulate the emotion. (If the emotion occurred while you were thinking, daydreaming, etc, please note this.) Then note the automatic thought associated with the emotion. Record the degree to which you believe this thought: 0% = not at all; 100% = completely. In rating degree of emotion: 1 = a trace; 100 = the most intense possible.

	Rational response 1. Write rational response to automatic thought(s). 2. Rate belief in rational response, 0–100 per cent.		**Outcome** 1. Re-rate belief in automatic thought(s), 0–100 per cent. 2. Specify and rate subsequent emotions, 0–100 per cent.
90%	It was inconvenient; she wouldn't be writing if she were angry about it.	95%	10% Guilty 20%
100%	I've done more than this before, and there is no law that says I have to get it all done.		25% Anxious 20%
100%	There is no evidence my boss will be angry, and even if he is I don't have to be upset.	100%	5% Anxious 10%
90%	I have got better in the past. Just because I think something doesn't make it true.		40% Sad 50%
100%	He asked me out for next weekend so he must like me. He probably did have to work. Even if he didn't like me it doesn't follow that *'no one* could *ever* like me.'	90%	30% Sad 40%

Date	Situation Describe: 1. Actual event leading to unpleasant emotion, or 2. Stream of thoughts, daydream, or recollection, leading to unpleasant emotion.	Emotions(s) 1. Specify sad; anxious; angry; etc. 2. Rate degree of emotion, 1–100 per cent.	Automatic thought(s) 1. Write automatic thought(s) that precede emotion(s) 2. Rate belief in automatic thought(s), 0–100 per cent.

Rational response 1. Write rational response to automatic thought(s). 2. Rate belief in rational response, 0–100 per cent.	Outcome 1. Re-rate belief in automatic thought(s), 0–100 per cent. 2. Specify and rate subsequent emotions, 0–100 per cent.

Beck Inventory

Name _____ Date _____

On this questionnaire are groups of statements. Please read each group of statements carefully. Then pick out the one statement in each group which best describes the way you have been feeling during the PAST WEEK, INCLUDING TODAY! Circle the number beside the statement you pick. If several statements in the group seem to apply equally well, circle each one. **Be sure to read all the statements in each group before making your choice.**

1   0   I do not feel sad.
    1   I feel sad.
    2   I am sad all the time and I can't snap out of it.
    3   I am so sad or unhappy that I can't stand it.

2   0   I am not particularly discouraged about the future.
    1   I feel discouraged about the future.
    2   I feel I have nothing to look forward to.
    3   I feel that the future is hopeless and that things cannot improve.

3   0   I do not feel like a failure.
    1   I feel I have failed more than the average person.
    2   As I look back on my life, all I can see is a lot of failures.
    3   I feel I am a complete failure as a person.

4   0   I get as much satisfaction out of things as I used to.
    1   I don't enjoy things the way I used to.
    2   I don't get real satisfaction out of anything anymore.
    3   I am dissatisfied or bored with everything.

5   0   I don't feel particularly guilty.
    1   I feel guilty a good part of the time.
    2   I feel quite guilty most of the time.
    3   I feel guilty all of the time.

6   0   I don't feel I am being punished.
    1   I feel I may be punished.

2 I expect to be punished.
3 I feel I am being punished.

7 0 I don't feel disappointed in myself.
1 I am disappointed in myself.
2 I am disgusted with myself.
3 I hate myself.

8 0 I don't feel I am any worse than anybody else.
1 I am critical of myself for my weaknesses or mistakes.
2 I blame myself all the time for my faults.
3 I blame myself for everything bad that happens.

9 0 I don't have any thoughts of killing myself.
1 I have thoughts of killing myself, but I would not carry them out.
2 I would like to kill myself.
3 I would kill myself if I had the chance.

10 0 I don't cry any more than usual.
1 I cry more now than I used to.
2 I cry all the time now.
3 I used to be able to cry, but now I can't cry even though I want to.

11 0 I am no more irritated now than I ever am.
1 I get annoyed or irritated more easily than I used to.
2 I feel irritated all the time now.
3 I don't get irritated at all by the things that used to irritate me.

12 0 I have not lost interest in other people.
1 I am less interested in other people than I used to be.
2 I have lost most of my interest in other people.
3 I have lost all of my interest in other people.

13 0 I make decisions about as well as I ever could.
1 I put off making decisions more than I used to.
2 I have greater difficulty in making decisions than before.
3 I can't make decisions at all anymore.

14 0 I don't feel I look any worse than I used to.
    1 I am worried that I am looking old or unattractive.
    2 I feel that there are permanent changes in my appearance that make me look unattractive.
    3 I believe that I look ugly.

15 0 I can work about as well as before.
    1 It takes an extra effort to get started at doing something.
    2 I have to push myself very hard to do anything.
    3 I can't do any work at all.

16 0 I can sleep as well as usual.
    1 I don't sleep as well as I used to.
    2 I wake up 1–2 hours earlier than usual and find it hard to get back to sleep.
    3 I wake up several hours earlier than I used to and cannot get back to sleep.

17 0 I don't get more tired than usual.
    1 I get tired more easily than I used to.
    2 I get tired from doing almost anything.
    3 I am too tired to do anything.

18 0 My appetite is no worse than usual.
    1 My appetite is not as good as it used to be.
    2 My appetite is much worse now.
    3 I have no appetite at all anymore.

19 0 I haven't lost much weight, if any, lately.
    1 I have lost more than 7 pounds.
    2 I have lost more than 10 pounds.
    3 I have lost more than 14 pounds.

20 0 I am no more worried about my health than usual.
    1 I am worried about physical problems such as aches and pains; or upset stomach; or constipation.
    2 I am very worried about physical problems and it's hard to think of much else.
    3 I am so worried about my physical problems that I cannot think about anything else.

21 0 I have not noticed any recent change in my interest in sex.
 1 I am less interested in sex than I used to be.
 2 I am much less interested in sex now.
 3 I have lost interest in sex completely.

Note. A score of approximately 21 or more for several weeks suggests that professional advice may help.

References

A T Beck, A J Rush, B F Shaw, G Emery, *Cognitive Therapy of Depression*, Guildford Press, New York (1979)

J Rush, *Beating Depression*, Century Hutchinson (1983)

D Burns, *Feeling Good: The New Mood Therapy*, Signet Press, New York (1981)

A Lakein, *How to Get Control of Your Time and Your Life*, Gower (1985)

P M Lewinsohn, R F Munoz, M A Youngren and A M Zeiss, *Control Your Depression*, Prentice Hall, Englewood Cliffs, New Jersey, USA (1978)

A D Kidman, 'Neurochemical and Cognitive Aspects of Depression', *Progress in Neurobiology*, Vol 24, pp 187–97 (1985)

CHAPTER 4
Risk Taking

Risk taking is important for the development and growth of both individuals and organisations. Unless we are prepared to take risks with respect to new ideas, new experiences, social interactions, then we will never know whether or not these things are helpful or enjoyable for us. The first person to eat an oyster took a risk but was presumably richly rewarded, and those of us who enjoy oysters are thankful.

Early experiences do not necessarily limit your potential. You can always learn new ways of acting, thinking and feeling. Your expectations can influence how successful you will be in your attempts to bring about change. If you are pessimistic, every time you start to implement change, you are telling yourself, 'What's the use, it's hopeless!' On the other hand, if you are more optimistic, you may well be telling yourself, 'Who knows? Maybe I can do it!' By being more optimistic, you can increase the chances that you will persist with a new activity and be successful at it. (These ideas are drawn from Albert Bandura's *Social Learning Theory*.)

Decision-making

Management experts such as Peter Drucker, Thomas Peters and Howard Stevenson argue that successful organisations encourage risk taking by their managers and entrepreneurial staff. Risk is implicit in all decisions, whether at work or at home, such as deciding whether or not to hire an applicant for a job or choosing which colour to paint the living room walls. All decisions can be wrong. Peter Drucker believes that too many of us look on a decision as a problem rather than as an opportunity.

As a result, we tend to settle for the solution with the lowest 'cost', even though it also promises the lowest gain. Every decision is an attempt to balance gain, cost and risk.

Another reason for fearing to make a decision and take a risk is that we may fail. We tend to be timid and conservative in so many of our activities and, as a result, both as individuals and as organisations, we can often stultify, keep doing the same old things and get nowhere. It is much easier and safer for us to stay with the familiar than to explore the unknown. This problem is dealt with in detail in Chapter 6 Fear of Failing.

The possibility of failure by individuals and organisations must be acknowledged so that when failure does occur we learn from it – we don't put ourselves down because of it, we then try something else. Often, we need to work at something to find out if we really did fail. An example would be having to speak in public, which produces great anxiety in many people. To clients who seek my advice about this problem I suggest that it is in their best interest to speak in public as often as they can before small and familiar groups to start with, and work up from there. Nevertheless, I argue, confront the anxiety-provoking situation, challenge it, take the risk and even if they appear foolish, tongue-tied and the audience bursts out laughing *they will not die*. Anxiety is the main cause of their self-defeating behaviour because they are telling themselves how awful it would be if they spoke badly. This will reduce to more manageable levels when they realise it is not despicable to speak badly in public, just unfortunate, and practice will make them better.

Fear of rejection

I would like to illustrate this by taking as an example a client in therapy who has taken risks. By risks, I am not suggesting foolish risks where people endanger their lives, but rather I am advising that people confront situations that are restricting their activities and ability to function.

One of the members of a depression group had problems meeting people. He was about to retire and felt lonely and isolated for a variety of reasons. He feared rejection very much and yet wanted to establish new friendships with women. I suggested that he take the risk of politely starting up conversations with a minimum of ten women during a week and, not only that, but *try to be rejected by at least five of them.*

This is actually a behavioural assignment and the paradoxical strategy here was to get him to seek out and experience rejection. By doing this he learnt that the anxiety associated with rejection was due to his thinking and that rejection in itself was not the horrifying experience he thought it was.

Rejection is a part of everyday life. Albert Ellis, the founder of rational-emotive therapy, related his own experiences as a young man when he was very fearful of women and of establishing any sort of relationship with a woman. He forced himself to make conversation with 120 women in a month by talking to them in the street, in supermarkets, going up and sitting beside them in the park. He related that more than half of them did not respond to his attempts at conversation, and they left. The remainder did, however, and about ten agreed to meet him again, but none of them reappeared. Now that may sound like an unpleasant experience, but he said that it taught him he could overcome his fear of speaking to the opposite sex, he had a number of pleasant and interesting conversations and subsequently had a number of very rewarding relationships.

Review rewarding activities

I see individuals and couples who are having relationship problems. I tell people who have been married or have lived together for long periods and who feel that a lot of the joy and excitement has gone that it is in their interests to take risks.

First, I suggest they do different things together, ask their friends what it is that they do and like, such as camping, sailing, riding, walking, learning golf, bridge, learning to swim, or more adventurous activities. At another level, if sex is dull and infrequent and they would like to increase their enjoyment, I suggest they try different times, techniques, places, to enhance the feelings that have waned and to use imagery to help focus on these feelings.

There are many activities that require effort, but because of the possibility of failure or even looking foolish in the eyes of others, there is a tendency to minimise risk-taking activities. I strongly suggest that people review the things in their lives that they enjoy, and more importantly, that they might enjoy. No matter what your age or handicaps, it is almost always possible to think of something new that you would like to try. I would not suggest that someone who hasn't exercised for 20 years should suddenly embark on a marathon run, but there are many other activities that you can try which would be potentially rewarding and exciting.

The pleasant events schedule

Peter Lewinsohn in his book *Control Your Depression* has devised a pleasant events schedule of over 300 items, which is given on pages 43–51, and he suggests that people review pleasant everyday activities so as to enrich their environment and to provide more rewarding experiences.

He argues that when we engage in very few activities which we experience as pleasant, we feel depressed. Also, when we feel depressed, we don't feel like engaging in the kinds of activity which are likely to be a source of pleasure and satisfaction for us. Not everyone reading this book feels depressed, but we can often feel bland, that life doesn't offer that much to us. The less we do, the more miserable and more negative we feel, and being down reduces our desire to take risks or try any new activities.

The approach I advocate here is to break that cycle and to find out what we really like doing. Lewinsohn lists such things as being in the country, talking about sport, playing golf, being naked, driving skilfully, laughing, playing tennis, being with animals, singing in a group, gambling, doing a project in your own way, being told you are needed, hiking, fishing and so the list goes on. Lewinsohn is a behaviour therapist working with people suffering from depression. He has found, after working with thousands of individuals, that this list represents activities within the reach of most people and which have been found to be most rewarding and pleasant.

Pleasant events schedule self-assessment form

The object of this exercise is to enable you to evaluate your current level of pleasant activities. This will help you to introduce changes in your life so that you can become aware of many potentially enjoyable activities and introduce and/or intensify some of these activities accordingly.

Filling in and scoring this questionnaire will take approximately two hours. The first part assesses how often these events have happened in your life in the past month.

How to fill in the form

Please indicate how often the events listed on pages 43–51 have occurred in the last month by rating each item in the frequency scale (Column F) as follows:

0: This has not happened in the past 30 days.
1: This has happened a few times (1–6) times in the past 30 days.
2: This has happened often (7 times or more) in the past 30 days.

Here is an example how you would do this. Item 4 is talking about sport. If you have talked about sport twice in the past 30 days, then you would mark 1 in column F next to item 4.

Some items include more than one event. For these items, mark how often you have done any of the events mentioned, for example, item 12 is Doing something artistic (painting, sculpture, drawing, video making, etc). You should rate item 12 on how often you have done anything artistic in the past month.

It is not expected that anyone will have done *all* of the 316 items in a single month!

The second part assesses how pleasant or rewarding each event was during the past month. To do this, rate each event in the pleasantness scale (column P).

0: This is not pleasant. (Use this rating for events which are neither neutral or unpleasant.)
1: This was somewhat pleasant. (Use this rating for events which were mildly or moderately pleasant.)

2: This was very pleasant. (Use this rating for events which were extremely pleasant.)

If an event has happened to you more than once in the past month, try to rate roughly how pleasant it was on average.

If an event has not happened to you during the past month, then rate it according to how much fun you think it would have been.

		F	P
1.	Being in the country	1	1
2.	Wearing expensive or formal clothes	0	1
3.	Making contributions to religious, charitable or other groups	1	2
4.	Talking about sport	1	1
5.	Meeting someone new of the same sex	1	2
6.	Taking tests when well prepared	0	2
7.	Going to a rock concert	0	1
8.	Playing cricket or softball	0	1
9.	Planning trips or holidays	1	1
10.	Buying things for myself	1	1
11.	Being at the beach	1	2
12.	Doing something artistic (painting, sculpture, drawing, making a video, etc)	2	2
13.	Rock climbing or mountaineering	0	2
14.	Reading the Scriptures or other sacred works	0	1
15.	Playing golf	0	1
16.	Taking part in military activities	0	0
17.	Rearranging or redecorating my room or house	2	2
18.	Being naked	2	2
19.	Going to a sports event	0	1
20.	Reading a 'How to do it' book or article	1	1
21.	Going to the races (horse, car, boat, etc)	0	1
22.	Reading stories, novels, poems or plays	2	2
23.	Going to a pub, restaurant, club, etc	2	1
24.	Going to lectures or hearing speakers	0	2
25.	Driving skilfully	0	2
26.	Breathing clean air	2	2
27.	Thinking up or arranging songs or music	0	2
28.	Getting drunk	2	1

	F	P
29. Saying something clearly	2	2
30. Boating (canoeing, sailing, etc)	0	2
31. Pleasing my parents	1	1
32. Restoring antiques, refinishing furniture, etc	2	2
33. Watching television	2	2
34. Talking to myself	2	2
35. Camping	0	0
36. Working in politics	0	0
37. Working on machines (cars, bikes, motorcycles, etc)	0	0
38. Thinking about something good in the future	2	2
39. Playing cards	2	2
40. Completing a difficult task	0	1
41. Laughing	2	2
42. Solving a problem puzzle, crossword, etc	2	2
43. Being at weddings, baptisms, confirmations, etc	0	1
44. Criticising someone	1	0
45. Shaving	2	2
46. Having lunch with friends or colleagues	0	2
47. Being coached	1	2
48. Playing tennis	0	1
49. Taking a shower	2	2
50. Driving long distances	2	2
51. Woodworking, carpentry	0	2
52. Writing stories, novels, plays or poetry	2	2
53. Being with animals	2	2
54. Picking flowers	0	2
55. Exploring (hiking away from known trails, etc)	0	2
56. Having a frank and open conversation	2	2
57. Singing in a group	0	2
58. Thinking about myself or my problems	2	2
59. Working on my job	1	2
60. Going to a party	0	1
61. Going to church functions (social gatherings, meetings, classes, bazaars, etc)	0	1
62. Speaking in a foreign language	0	1
63. Going to service, civic, or social club meetings	0	1
64. Going to a business meeting or a conference	0	1
65. Being in a sporty or expensive car	0	1
66. Playing a musical instrument	0	2

		F	P
67.	Making snacks	2	2
68.	Skiing	0	1
69.	Being helped	2	2
70.	Wearing informal clothes	2	2
71.	Combing or brushing my hair	2	2
72.	Acting	2	2
73.	Taking a nap	2	0
74.	Being with friends	2	2
75.	Pickling, freezing, making preserves, etc	0	1
76.	Driving fast	0	0
77.	Solving a personal problem	2	2
78.	Being in a city	2	2
79.	Taking a bath	2	2
80.	Singing to myself	2	0
81.	Making food or crafts to sell or give away	0	0
82.	Playing snooker or billiards	2	0
83.	Being with my grandchildren	0	2
84.	Playing chess or draughts	0	1
85.	Practising a craft (pottery, jewellery, leatherwork, beadwork, weaving, etc)	0	1
86.	Weighing myself	1	1
87.	Scratching myself	1	1
88.	Putting on make-up, doing my hair, etc	1	1
89.	Designing or doing technical drawing	2	2
90.	Visiting people who are sick, bedridden, housebound or in trouble	0	2
91.	Cheering at a sports or some other event	0	2
92.	Bowling	0	2
93.	Being popular at a gathering	1	1
94.	Watching wild animals	2	0
95.	Having an original idea	2	2
96.	Gardening or landscaping	0	1
97.	Looking at the stars or the moon	2	2
98.	Reading essays or technical, academic or professional literature	1	2
99.	Wearing new clothes	1	2
100.	Dancing	1	2
101.	Sitting in the sun	0	1
102.	Riding a motorcycle	0	0

	F	P
103. Just sitting and thinking	2	2
104. Social drinking	2	2
105. Seeing good things happen to family and friends	2	2
106. Going to a fair, carnival, circus, zoo or amusement park	0	2
107. Talking about philosophy or religion	2	1
108. Gambling	0	0
109. Planning or organising something	1	1
110. Glue sniffing	0	0
111. Having a drink by myself	0	0
112. Listening to the sounds of nature	1	2
113. Going out with a member of the opposite sex	2	2
114. Having a lively talk	2	2
115. Racing in a car, motorcycle, boat, etc	0	0
116. Listening to the radio	2	1
117. Having friends come to visit	1	2
118. Playing in a sporting competition	0	0
119. Introducing people I think would like each other	2	2
120. Giving gifts	2	2
121. Going to school meetings, political rallies, court sessions, etc	0	1
122. Getting massages or backrubs	2	2
123. Getting letters, cards or notes	2	2
124. Watching the sky, clouds or a storm	2	2
125. Going on outings (to the park, a picnic, a barbecue, etc)	0	1
126. Playing squash, tennis, golf, netball, etc	0	1
127. Buying something for my family	2	2
128. Photography	0	2
129. Giving a speech or lecture	0	2
130. Reading maps	0	0
131. Gathering natural objects (wild fruit, rocks, driftwood, etc)	0	2
132. Working on my finances	1	1
133. Wearing clean clothes	2	1
134. Making a major purchase or investment (car, expensive equipment, house, shares, etc)	0	1
135. Helping someone	2	2
136. Being in the mountains	0	2

F P

137. Getting on well in my job (being promoted, given a rise, or offered a better job, etc) ☐ ☐
138. Hearing jokes ☐ ☐
139. Winning a bet ☐ ☐
140. Talking about my children or my grandchildren ☐ ☐
141. Meeting someone new of the opposite sex ☐ ☐
142. Going to Christian mission or crusade ☐ ☐
143. Talking about my health ☐ ☐
144. Seeing beautiful scenery ☐ ☐
145. Eating good meals ☐ ☐
146. Improving my health (having my teeth seen to, getting new glasses, changing my diet, etc) ☐ ☐
147. Being in the centre of town ☐ ☐
148. Wrestling or boxing ☐ ☐
149. Hunting or shooting ☐ ☐
150. Playing in a musical group ☐ ☐
151. Hiking ☐ ☐
152. Going to a museum or exhibition ☐ ☐
153. Writing papers, essays, articles, reports, memos, etc ☐ ☐
154. Doing a job well ☐ ☐
155. Having spare time ☐ ☐
156. Fishing ☐ ☐
157. Lending something ☐ ☐
158. Being noticed as sexually attractive ☐ ☐
159. Pleasing employers, teachers, etc ☐ ☐
160. Counselling someone ☐ ☐
161. Going to a health club, sauna, etc ☐ ☐
162. Having someone criticise me ☐ ☐
163. Learning to do something new ☐ ☐
164. Going to a fast-food restaurant (Kentucky Fried Chicken, McDonald's, etc) ☐ ☐
165. Complimenting or praising someone ☐ ☐
166. Thinking about people I like ☐ ☐
167. Being at a club (sport, special interest, etc) ☐ ☐
168. Taking revenge on someone ☐ ☐
169. Being with my parents ☐ ☐
170. Horse riding ☐ ☐
171. Protesting about social, political, or environmental conditions ☐ ☐

	F	P
172. Talking on the telephone	☐	☐
173. Having daydreams	☐	☐
174. Kicking leaves, sand, pebbles, etc	☐	☐
175. Playing lawn sports (badminton, croquet, bowls, etc)	☐	☐
176. Going to school and college reunions, etc	☐	☐
177. Seeing famous people	☐	☐
178. Going to see a film	☐	☐
179. Kissing	☐	☐
180. Being alone	☐	☐
181. Organising my time	☐	☐
182. Cooking meals	☐	☐
183. Being praised by people I admire	☐	☐
184. Outwitting a 'superior'	☐	☐
185. Feeling the presence of the Lord in my life	☐	☐
186. Doing a project in my own way	☐	☐
187. Doing odd jobs around the house	☐	☐
188. Crying	☐	☐
189. Being told I am needed	☐	☐
190. Being at a family reunion or get-together	☐	☐
191. Giving a party	☐	☐
192. Washing my hair	☐	☐
193. Coaching someone	☐	☐
194. Going to a restaurant	☐	☐
195. Seeing or smelling a flower or plant	☐	☐
196. Being invited out	☐	☐
197. Receiving honours (civic, military, etc)	☐	☐
198. Using toilet water, perfume, or aftershave	☐	☐
199. Having someone agree with me	☐	☐
200. Reminiscing, talking about old times	☐	☐
201. Getting up early in the morning	☐	☐
202. Experiencing peace and quiet	☐	☐
203. Carrying out experiments or other scientific work	☐	☐
204. Visiting friends	☐	☐
205. Writing in a diary	☐	☐
206. Playing football	☐	☐
207. Being counselled	☐	☐
208. Saying prayers	☐	☐
209. Giving massages or backrubs	☐	☐

F   P

210. Hitchhiking ☐ ☐
211. Meditating or doing yoga ☐ ☐
212. Seeing a fight ☐ ☐
213. Doing favours for people ☐ ☐
214. Talking with people at work or in my class at school ☐ ☐

215. Being relaxed ☐ ☐
216. Being asked for my help or advice ☐ ☐
217. Thinking about other people's problems ☐ ☐
218. Playing board games (Monopoly, Scrabble, etc) ☐ ☐
219. Sleeping soundly at night ☐ ☐
220. Doing heavy outdoor work (cutting or chopping wood, clearing land, farm work, etc) ☐ ☐

221. Reading the newspaper ☐ ☐
222. Shocking people, swearing, making obscene gestures, etc ☐ ☐
223. Motocross ☐ ☐
224. Being in a body-awareness, sensitivity, encounter, therapy, or other such group ☐ ☐

225. Dreaming at night ☐ ☐
226. Playing table tennis ☐ ☐
227. Brushing my teeth ☐ ☐
228. Swimming ☐ ☐
229. Being in a fight ☐ ☐
230. Running, jogging or doing gymnastics ☐ ☐
231. Walking barefoot ☐ ☐
232. Playing with a frisbee or throwing a ball ☐ ☐
233. Doing housework or laundry, cleaning things ☐ ☐
234. Being with my flat mate ☐ ☐
235. Listening to music ☐ ☐
236. Arguing ☐ ☐
237. Knitting, crocheting, embroidery or intricate needlework ☐ ☐

238. Petting, necking ☐ ☐
239. Amusing people ☐ ☐
240. Talking about sex ☐ ☐
241. Going to a hairdresser or beautician ☐ ☐
242. Having people to stay ☐ ☐
243. Being with someone I love ☐ ☐

	F	P
244. Reading magazines	☐	☐
245. Sleeping late	☐	☐
246. Starting a new project	☐	☐
247. Being stubborn	☐	☐
248. Having sexual relations	☐	☐
249. Having other sexual gratification	☐	☐
250. Going to the library	☐	☐
251. Playing rugby, hockey, etc	☐	☐
252. Preparing a new or special food	☐	☐
253. Birdwatching	☐	☐
254. Shopping	☐	☐
255. Watching people	☐	☐
256. Building or watching a fire	☐	☐
257. Winning an argument	☐	☐
258. Selling or trading something	☐	☐
259. Going to see a play	☐	☐
260. Confessing or apologising	☐	☐
261. Repairing things	☐	☐
262. Working with others as a team	☐	☐
263. Bicycling	☐	☐
264. Telling people what to do	☐	☐
265. Being happy with people	☐	☐
266. Playing party games	☐	☐
267. Writing letters, cards or notes	☐	☐
268. Talking about politics or public affairs	☐	☐
269. Asking for help or advice	☐	☐
270. Going to banquets, lunches, etc	☐	☐
271. Talking about my hobby or special interest	☐	☐
272. Watching attractive women or men	☐	☐
273. Smiling at people	☐	☐
274. Playing in sand, a stream, the grass, etc	☐	☐
275. Talking about other people	☐	☐
276. Being with my husband or wife	☐	☐
277. Having people show interest in what I have said	☐	☐
278. Going on field trips, nature walks, etc	☐	☐
279. Expressing my love to someone	☐	☐
280. Smoking cigarettes, cigars, etc	☐	☐
281. Caring for houseplants	☐	☐
282. Having coffee, tea, etc with friends	☐	☐

F P

283. Going for a walk
284. Collecting things
285. Playing squash, etc
286. Sewing
287. Suffering for a good cause
288. Remembering a departed friend or loved one, visiting the cemetery
289. Beachcombing
290. Being complimented or told I have done well
291. Being told I am loved
292. Eating snacks
293. Staying up late
294. Having family members or friends do something that makes me proud of them
295. Being with my children
296. Going to auctions, jumble sales, etc
297. Thinking about an interesting question
298. Doing voluntary work, working on community service projects
299. Water-skiing, surfing, diving, windsurfing, etc
300. Receiving money
301. Defending or protecting someone, stopping fraud or abuse
302. Hearing a good sermon
303. Picking up a hitchhiker
304. Winning a competion
305. Making a new friend
306. Talking about my job or school
307. Reading cartoons, comic strips or comic books
308. Borrowing something
309. Travelling with a group
310. Seeing old friends
311. Teaching someone
312. Using my strength
313. Travelling
314. Going to office parties or department get-togethers
315. Attending a concert, opera, or ballet
316. Playing with pets

Assessing the results of your completed questionnaire

After you have rated each item on frequency and pleasantness you are now ready to do some calculations.

Add up all the frequency ratings (those figures you put in column F) and divide the total by 316. This is your mean frequency score.

Add up all the pleasantness ratings (those figures you put in column P) and divide the total by 316. This is your mean pleasantness score.

Compare your scores with those shown in the table below:

	Average ranges	
Age group	*Mean frequency score*	*Mean pleasantness score*
20–39	0.63–1.03	0.86–1.26
40–59	0.57–0.97	0.82–1.22
60 or older	0.50–0.90	0.78–1.18

By comparing your score with the average range for your age group, you can evaluate yourself. If your mean frequency score is equal to or lower than the lower end of the average range, you are definitely low, which indicates that you are not engaging in activities to the extent that a lot of people your age do. Similarly, with your mean pleasantness score. If it is low, it means that at present there are relatively few activities that are likely to be a source of pleasure to you. If your score is high, it means that, potentially, you have a large number of activities and events from which you could derive satisfaction.

Thus, by examining your own mean score against the average and the various values you have given to events – particularly from the pleasantness score – you will have reliable information from which you can make decisions about changing the frequency of certain activities that you are now doing in your life – reducing some, increasing others and, more importantly, introducing activities that you consider to be very pleasant and rewarding.

Mood-changing activities

Through various experiments, it has been found that there is a special group of activities that make people feel good when they engage in them. These activities fall into three types:

- social interactions in which the person feels wanted, liked, respected, understood, appreciated and accepted (for example, being with happy people, having people show interest in what you have said, thinking about people you like, being with friends)
- activities associated with feelings of adequacy, competence and independence (for example, doing a project in your own way, planning or organising something, doing a job well, learning to do something new)
- activities that are intrinsically pleasant (for example, laughing, being relaxed, eating good meals, thinking about something good in the future, seeing beautiful scenery, experiencing peace and quiet, sleeping soundly at night).

These are the activities that I particularly emphasise for people who are feeling depressed.

Planning

I suggest that, after studying the schedule of pleasant events, clients write down activities that they would like to do. Then they should include an increasing number of pleasant activities in their daily lives and note how this changes their sense of enjoyment, well-being and feelings about others over a period of weeks.

Together with this review of potentially enjoyable activities, I strongly urge a review of both long- and short-term goals. This is important because most people have never done this on paper. I never suggest that these goals are unchangeable – it is more an exercise to help people clarify their objectives. It requires time, paper and a pen and careful thinking about what you really want to do with your life in the next six months, the next three years and until you die, and to list the sort of things you would like to pursue. Then it is critical to assign some priorities to these goals.

Using Alan Lakein's method from his book *How to Get Control of Your Time and Your Life*, you assign an A to any high-value goal, a B to a lesser-value goal and a C to a low-value goal. Now look carefully at all the A values or high-priority goals and give them a numerical rating – A1, A2, etc. At the end of the exercise, perhaps two or three domestic and work-related goals will emerge as the top priority ones.

Then, on another piece of paper, you list the steps to be taken to achieve a particular goal. You rarely achieve a goal by just doing one thing – a series of steps needs to be taken. Many of these goals include potentially rewarding activities, but often they require hard work, such as having to take a course, travel long distances for lessons, long hours writing a book or play. More details are given in Chapter 8, Personal Organisation.

Many of these activities require risk taking to learn them, to invite others to participate, and to do them. They may even require some short-term frustration, such as learning to swim, even though you may be 20 years older than all the other people learning. However, once you have learned, you can then learn to surf, or canoe or any other water sport without fear of drowning. You can swim in rivers and lakes and are capable of saving your own or someone else's life if you are in a boating accident. You can feel more confident about your capacities in general.

You feel the way you think

Human beings have a remarkable tendency to defeat themselves by their thinking, their feelings and their behaviour. The types of thought that prevent us from enjoying life more are, 'What will other people think if I suddenly decide to take guitar and singing lessons, they might think I'm trying to show off, or that I haven't got the voice or ability to pick out different notes'. Other self-defeating thoughts include, 'I will appear foolish', 'I am too old', 'This isn't for me', whereas even if you *do* appear somewhat foolish or incongruous, you can say to yourself, 'Too bad, I can improve with practice, however, if I never try then I will never know.'

A prescription for enjoyment

I would like to list some specific actions you can take to make your life more enjoyable.

- Try to find some person or things in which you can honestly get absorbed for their own sake and not for 'ego enhancing' reasons. It is perfectly acceptable to love your own children and your spouse or to devote yourself to helping others in one of the caring professions, such as teaching, nursing, medicine. Nevertheless you also have the perfect right as a human being to devote yourself to something such as chess or bridge, which has relatively little altruistic value. You probably won't love anyone or anything very deeply unless you have the courage of your convictions. Do not always follow others and do the things they want to do, just because you want their approval.

- In taking risks with new fields of endeavour, try to choose a challenging long-term project, rather than something simple or short-term. Most intelligent people will not remain *wholly* absorbed in simply making a sexual conquest, playing dominoes or weight-lifting for very long because they can master these things within a given time and then find them boring and unchallenging. Rather, try to select a goal such as writing a play or a story, making a significant contribution to your community, or achieving or maintaining a long-term relationship. This kind of activity may well remain intriguing for a long time to come.

- Don't expect vital absorption to develop quickly, because inertia, fear of failure or ignorance of the true depths of a given subject often cause us to give up. You may at first have to push yourself forcibly into a certain field of endeavour and make yourself stick at it for a reasonable time before you really begin to get absorbed in it and fascinated by it. Before you conclude that you definitely do not enjoy a given project, give it an honest, fairly prolonged try. Then if you still don't like it you can look around for a different kind of absorbing activity.

- Think about varying your interests and having some important peripheral projects as well; even if you get absorbed in some major endeavour, it may not last for ever. You can thrive on a variety of goals but you can easily go stale if you only concentrate on one pursuit. If, therefore, you can vary your reading, your hobbies, the organisations to which you belong and your circle of friends, you are likely to remain more vital, more alive than if you routinely keep doing the same thing over and over again. This implies revising long- and short-term goals and continually being on the alert for new activities, new risk-taking ventures.

- It requires action to overcome inertia. Often you can make yourself undertake specific acts of courage: raise a difficult issue with an employer at the office, ask a very attractive person out, take your idea for a book to a publisher. Keep forcing yourself into action long enough and often enough until the action itself proves easier and even, eventually, enjoyable.

- Try adopting a different role for a time and force yourself to live up to this assumed role. If you are normally shy and retiring, and for a week can act as one of the most outgoing and assertive individuals you know, you may find it relatively easy after acting out that role, to be less inhibited. The more you can force yourself to do something you feel you are sure you cannot do, the more you may prove your certainty wrong and show yourself that you can do it.

- Try some regular role-playing for yourself, particularly in the form of assertiveness training where you push yourself to do 'daring things' you normally refuse to do, eg starting up conversations with interesting people at the theatre, supermarket or on the train, auditioning for acting roles in amateur theatricals, giving a talk to your parents' and teachers' association on a topic that you feel is important, go on an assault course.

Living in this society with interactions and competition between family members, friends and colleagues often produces conflict. Our tendencies to want to appear always successful and clever in front of others and to want the world to be a harmonious, perfect place, when it isn't, will inevitably bring about self-disturbance. Anxiety will immobilise and prevent us from taking those chances which are important to our enjoyment and growth as human beings.

References

P Drucker, *The Effective Executive*, Pan (1970)

H H Stevenson & D Gumpert, 'The Heart of Entrepreneurship' *Harvard Business Review*, Vol. 63 (1985) pp 85–94

T J Peters and R H Waterman, *In Search of Excellence*, Chapter 7, 'Autonomy and Entrepreneurship', Harper & Row (1982)

P Lewinsohn, R F Munoz, M A Youngren, A M Zeiss, *Control Your Depression*, Prentice-Hall, Englewood Cliffs, New Jersey, USA (1978)

R Alex Mackenzie, *The Time Trap*, Chapter 6 'Handling Decisions', McGraw-Hill (1975)

A Ellis & R A Harper, *A New Guide to Rational Living*, Wilshire, North Hollywood, California, USA (1975)

A Bandura, *Social Learning Theory*, Prentice-Hall, Englewood Cliffs, New Jersey, USA (1977)

CHAPTER 5
Frustration – Make it Work for You

Recently I was talking to one of my students who said he just couldn't stand studying any more. I asked him what he meant by this and he said that he was unable to face up to his text books, to take pen to paper and he didn't see himself passing at the end of the year. I agreed with the last statement but not with the first or second. I said, 'What do you mean, you cannot stand studying any more? Of course you can, it's just that right now you find it quite unpleasant, inconvenient, frustrating, but if I offered to write out a cheque to you for £1000 if you would go immediately to the library and study for three hours would you do so?' He agreed he would under those conditions, but not at the moment. I pointed out that it was not true to say that he *could not* study but rather that he wasn't sufficiently motivated to overcome the quite high frustration barriers that had built up.

Low frustration tolerance

Low frustration tolerance (LFT) is a common problem. It occurs frequently in young people and, unfortunately, also in many adults. What does it mean? It means that we are telling ourselves in our minds that things should be as we want them to be and that the world owes us contentment and happiness. This is a totally irrational idea and when it doesn't happen we get angry, anxious, demanding, blaming the world and the people in it for these undesirable circumstances. I suggest that it is quite rational to vigorously pursue the goals of contentment and happiness but, when bad events happen, not to worsen the situation by being incredibly anxious, angry and blaming others.

A fundamental principle of living in a world full of people with different interests and goals is that there will inevitably be frustration and pain from time to time. Some people will have much more to tolerate than others. Daily living means interaction between our highly developed senses and the outside world and, at times, this will be unpleasant. It is therefore in our interests to learn how to deal as effectively as we can with unpleasant and inconvenient situations. They include such things as sickness, financial problems, behaviour of others, boredom, pain and climatic conditions, such as heat, cold and humidity. Even the rich and famous have frustrations. Consider Brigitte Bardot at 50, living alone with her cats, depressed about growing old and her apparently unsatisfactory relationships; David Niven having to deal with motor neurone disease from which he ultimately died; Sigmund Freud who for 15 years fought cancer of the jaw and palate, was subjected to 33 operations and yet continued working and seeing patients until almost the day he died.

We all know people who seem to handle frustration and discomfort better than others. We know it in ourselves when we have 'good' days and cope with an incident such as being criticised unfairly with no chance to reply, or waiting in an interminable queue at a bank or being subjected to abuse while driving. You can react to these situations aggressively, protesting, swearing, heart racing, perspiring, risking an accident or even physical assault, or you can accept that there is very little you can do in some situations and that you may as well make the best of it. I'm not suggesting that everything that happens to you should be accepted. There are many situations where appropriate assertive behaviour can relieve the frustration or change the circumstances, but then there are many others where very little can be done, such as being caught in a traffic jam, and, unless you are willing to put other people's lives at risk and break the law by driving on the wrong side of the road you just have to stay there.

Emotion and pain

The Roman philosopher, Epictetus, said that, 'Men are disturbed not by things, but by the view which they take of them.' Modern writers, like Ronald Melzak in his book, *The Puzzle of Pain*, have shown that physical pain is experienced and reacted to, not only in relation to the intensity of the painful stimulus but largely in relation to the subjective, individual, attitudes of the person who is suffering. Again, this doesn't mean that you seek out painful situations or do nothing to avert them, but that you do not make yourself worse by refusing to accept that there will be painful experiences from time to time.

Magda Arnold in her book, *Emotion and Personality* said that it is not really the frustration itself, but one's subjective and moralistic attitude towards this frustration that causes the hostility, aggression or depression, reactions that so often occur. Albert Allis, the founder of Rational-Emotive Therapy, argues this even more forcefully with his concept of the irrational belief system and self-image that people have of themselves (see page 17).

In my psychotherapy practice, I argue as strongly as I can with clients to dispute their irrational ideas. I say it is not in their interests to worsen their negative feelings about a frustrating situation, but rather to see it as a challenge and a learning experience from which they can benefit in the future.

The value of frustration

A common question I get asked is, 'What good is frustration?' My answer is that it is only of value depending upon your attitude towards it. With a rational attitude frustration can:

- help you to learn how to control your demanding tendencies, which almost all humans have for things to be perfect in an imperfect world;
- help you to learn to deal with a difficult situation, and knowing you have handled it fairly well, you are in a better position to manage frustrations that will occur in the future;
- help you to appreciate and enjoy pleasant events in your life much more.

If there were no unpleasantness in our existence then we would have nothing with which to compare enjoyable activities. Anyone who has spent time in hospital, studying intensively or working particularly hard under difficult circumstances knows how enjoyable it is when that time has passed. How nice it is to be able to walk around a garden or through a forest when one has been in a hospital bed for several weeks; how pleasant it is to meet with family and friends after an intense period of work or a long absence.

Frustration can work *for* you. It's in your own interests to make use of it, to develop your skills in handling it and to show to others, especially your children or your fellow workers, how to manage the inevitable frustrations that occur with living. Practising this type of attitude reduces feelings of frustration and your actions will be noticed by others who can learn from you.

References

R Melzak, *The Puzzle of Pain*, Penguin, (OP) (1977)

M Arnold, *Emotion and Personality* Columbia University Press, New York (1960)

M J Smith, *When I Say No I Feel Guilty*, Bantam, (1976)

A Ellis and R A Harper, *A New Guide to Rational Living*, Wilshire, North Hollywood, California, USA (1975)

CHAPTER 6
Fear of Failing

This chapter, together with the next three, Hostility at Work, Personal Organisation and Coping With Change, was written originally for managers, but the principles can be applied to any situation at home, at school or as a member of an organisation.

We all learn very early in life that failing is bad and many of us then take this to mean that if we fail we are less worthy human beings. It occurs in school where marks are assigned for exams and projects and students compete to be first in their class; in sporting activities where individuals are striving to become the best at swimming, tennis, running or football.

The reality is that very few of us can achieve these top grades but we take notice of others – our friends, parents, brothers, sisters and teachers – who, by their attitudes and remarks, generate feelings of worthlessness when we don't meet their expectations.

Then when people start work they often find themselves in a climate of competitiveness, hostility and jealousy. This, together with the experiences they have had at school, can further undermine their confidence. Many working people often experience these feelings.

Decision-making

According to Peter Drucker, an eminent writer in the field of management, effective workers and especially managers make many decisions. Vilfredo Pareto told us in the nineteenth century that about 80 per cent of all the things we do are relatively unimportant and produce only 20 per cent of results.

Consequently, the decision-making should be concentrated on that other 20 per cent that produces 80 per cent of results. Decisions on most issues can be made quickly, but the productive and important decisions should be identified and considered carefully.

The other great problem we all face, managers or not, is the fear of making the wrong decision and the 'failure' label that others and ourselves would attach to the decision. Good managers are risk takers, and implicit in any risk taking is the chance of failure. No one will alway be right but that does not mean that they will always be wrong either. However, unless staff and the organisations they work for accept that occasionally wrong decisions will be made, managers will never take the risks that are necessary for the organisation to succeed.

Drucker argues that managers should see decision-making as a challenge rather than a problem and they should not settle for the solution with the lowest cost, even though it also promises the lowest risk. Every decision is an attempt to balance gains, costs and risks. If management is to motivate through challenge it must insist on risk taking, which involves a distinct possibility of failure.

My experience has been that people learn on the job by making mistakes and good workers don't repeat their mistakes very often – it is one of the most effective learning processes. The same principles can be applied to managing a home and family.

The principle of parity

These attitudes that we have about ourselves and failure are the key reason for the self-defeating behaviour of many people at work. Again I would argue the principle of parity – that *we are essentially equal to one another*, and there are no superior human beings. Rather, there are people who are very good at certain activities, but this does not make them superior human beings. This principle directly contradicts the common irrational idea that many of us have that we must succeed in everything we do and gain the approval of all significant others for our actions. That idea, more than anything else, will make us anxious and disturbed when we fail. The reality is that it is impossible to succeed in that fashion, yet we find executives at 45 becoming depressed that they are not going to achieve the position they wanted, or their business is not going to make them millionaires. Then they become depressed about their depression and feel even more of a failure. This generates a spiral of self-defeating thoughts and behaviour that just gets worse and worse. Their performance suffers because of their beliefs about themselves.

We have many more things going for us than we realise and, in order to break this cycle, a written analysis of our activities and achievements to date can help. Much can be gained by looking at all facets of one's life as a parent, husband, wife, adviser of others, listener, humorist, handyman, gardener, card player, conversationalist, friend, rather than categorising oneself as the person who failed to become the top dog.

Self-acceptance

The principle of self-acceptance is important. Rather than people talking about self-esteem and self-approval, I prefer not to use these terms, but to concentrate on self-acceptance: 'I fully accept myself merely because I decide to fully accept myself and I do not need any special reason to do it.' I am saying that people should not rate themselves as human beings on the basis of their behaviour. Rather, when we or others do things that we consider stupid or immoral we do them because we are too ignorant, foolish or emotionally disturbed to stop ourselves. We often cause unhappiness and even harm to others because of our acts. However, a bad act does not make a bad person; it tells a person that, for his sake as well as for others, it would be highly preferable to change, otherwise he might lose his friends, alienate his family or colleagues or, depending on the act, go to gaol.

This doesn't mean that you will not strive and do all in your power to improve your performance as a student, salesperson, husband, wife or whatever, but, when failures occur in these roles, as they inevitably will, you do not then downgrade and condemn yourself.

Recently at a seminar I conducted on interpersonal

relationships at work, one of the participants made a comment that I feel sums up the position quite nicely: 'I may have failed at a particular activity, but I myself am not a failure.'

References

A Ellis, *Effective Leadership: A Rational Approach*, Institute for Rational-Emotive Therapy, New York (1972)

P Drucker, *The Effective Executive*, Pan (1970)

CHAPTER 7
Hostility at Work

Anyone who works for a public or private enterprise, be it large or small, at some time or other will have to face up to hostility and aggression from colleagues, superiors or subordinates. The frequency varies enormously, and some unfortunate individuals are forced to tolerate an almost continuously hostile environment. Individuals react in a variety of ways, countering aggression with aggression, or alternatively withdrawing, becoming depressed and/or excessively anxious. Hostility exists in organisations because people are competing for promotion, remuneration, power and because of the personalities involved. The reasons for people being aggressive are complex but not very helpful for someone who is trying to deal with a hostile co-worker.

The need for approval and justice

Two irrational ideas that are prevalent and which contribute to self-defeating behaviour are:

- that you *must* succeed in everything you do and gain the approval of all important people for these actions;
- that you *must* be treated with complete fairness and justice at all times by employers and others and if this does not occur, 'they' are awful individuals who must be punished.

Another problem is that you do not choose the people you work with. Very often you join a company and have to work with some people you would normally avoid.

Hostile and aggressive behaviour occurs frequently at work

and some advantages accrue to people who display these tendencies. They are able to frighten other people and so perhaps get them to do things for them. Some people believe that by becoming aggressive, you display leadership qualities and you gain the respect of others by 'coming on strong'. This may reinforce a perception of themselves as strong, tough individuals who achieve results no matter what the cost to others.

The disadvantages, which I believe outweigh the advantages of such behaviour, include very little feedback or false feedback from your subordinates, together with hostility that is aroused towards you because of your aggression. It may not be direct, but rather by passive aggressive behaviour which means staff deliberately undermine colleagues whom they fear and dislike. Hostility generates anger and because people do not think as rationally or as clearly when they are angry, they often say and do things they later regret. Many people who are aggressive cause stress and anxiety in others and, in many cases, upon reflection, in themselves. The chronic effects of stress and anxiety upon general health are discussed in Chapter 11.

Techniques for controlling anger

If you decide that your aggressive behaviour towards your colleagues is something you would like to change, then I would offer some suggestions drawn from the cognitive restructuring techniques of the psychologists Arnold Lazarus and Albert Ellis, which have already been mentioned in Chapter 6, Fear of Failing.

The first is the concept of parity which is that we are essentially equal to one another. There are no superior human beings, there are just people who are very good at certain activities, be it management, writing, speaking and so on, but this does not make them superior to others. We are all fallible and vulnerable, with limitations as well as assets.

The next point is to accept that often and, perhaps frequently, the behaviour of others will be bad and that they will do things that you consider very disappointing. However, this does not reduce their value as human beings. It just means that we will, from time to time, do things that are extremely annoying to each other, as we have done for as long as people have lived and worked together in groups. We will also do unexpected things, and it is these behaviour patterns that we do not approve of, but have to learn to cope with and accept.

Instead of becoming extremely angry and perhaps even abusive with a person you discover has lied about certain things within the company, it would be better to change your response from outrage to one of annoyance and disappointment. Learn to accept the fact that, from time to time, we do lie and will continue to do so. Of course, you may be able to take some appropriate action to assertively, but not aggressively, point out this failing and clarify future action, penalising those who break rules.

Another example to illustrate this point would be two employees who are appointed at about the same time with the same qualifications, both working hard. Let us say you are one of them and you find out that your colleague has been promoted, in your eyes, quite unjustifiably to a higher post. A typical reaction would be to get furious, perhaps spend a lot of time feeling resentful about the management and even plotting and scheming to defeat and block your colleague in his new position. People often refuse to communicate under these circumstances, refuse to cooperate and not only waste a great deal of their own time but that of other members of the company. Consequently, they reduce their own effectiveness in the job they are doing. This is not to say that you should be happy about what has happened, quite the reverse. It is appropriate for you to be disappointed and to want things to be different but, given that it has happened, *it is not in your interests* now to engage in self-defeating behaviour that can only worsen your own position and lessen your chances for future advancement.

'Hot' and 'cool' thoughts

A method I recommend to clients who see me with problems about controlling their anger is to use the Daily Record Dysfunctional Thoughts Form on pages 30–33 and to write down the situation that provoked their anger response.

Let's say that a colleague regularly leaves his job early and you are left to cope, not only with your work, but some of his work as well and the closing up of the office. Your anger response, or 'hot thoughts' might be, 'That so and so, how dare he go on like that and leave me to do his work as well as my work. He is a lazy, good-for-nothing individual and I'm going to get even with him somehow or other.' Over a period of time your anger can build up to almost the 100 per cent level.

A 'cool thought' about this situation might be, 'Well, he does that because he doesn't understand the rules and he appears to be an insensitive person whose work performance is not particularly good anyway. I'm going to take some action to change this as soon as possible, but I am not going to allow myself to become so upset that I can't even do my own work, lose sleep over the problem and make myself sick in the stomach every time I see him.' Just by writing down that 'cool thought', or rational response, you can reduce your anger substantially to a level of appropriate annoyance.

Some people find it useful to quickly write down on a memo pad 'hot' and 'cool' thoughts in columns and to do a quick cost-benefit analysis of their anger.

A 'difficult' superior

Another example would be an aggressive, difficult superior. If you talk with groups of managers, as I do, you will find that many of them are dealing with this type of person. Sometimes it is not possible to change jobs immediately or move to a new post within the company, and it is a matter of perhaps tolerating this situation until a suitable position arises (especially at time of high unemployment).

The cognitive restructuring technique of Dr Ellis suggests that in such a situation you should accept that this person's behaviour is not going to change, but also recognise that your reactions to it of anxiety, depression, hostility are not helpful to you and therefore you should modify them as much as possible. This, I emphasise, does not mean that you succumb, that you become passive and meek, but rather that you are not going to allow your reactions to this undesirable behaviour to disturb you, to affect your work, your sleep and perhaps your family life. Thus, if you can change your reactions to a particular situation, this change in behaviour in many cases, though not all, produces change in the person who is causing the problem. It will also result in a reduction of self-destructive behaviour because people who think too deeply about what was said and done in a particular situation and what they *should* have said and done during an anxious, and tense exchange, get further upset about their own anxiety and tension and do themselves no good. Your change of attitude will, if nothing else, enable you to tolerate the stress of the situation more effectively and decide what suitable steps can be taken in a calmer, more rational frame of mind.

Is anger ever appropriate?

Often I am asked, 'Is it never appropriate to get really angry?', and I reply that the words 'never' and 'always' I try to avoid. It can be appropriate on certain occasions for anger to be adaptive, that is, useful to achieve your goal. For instance, if your young children are crossing the road without looking, it may well be that angry words would be in order to prevent an accident and firmly instil in the children's memory the danger of such action. In the case of self-defence, anger and violence may be the only response in order to save yourself from serious injury. However, apart from these examples, most daily interactions between people do not require the angry, hostile responses that we so often see and hear that lead to so much stress, especially at work.

I believe it is very important for people at all levels, but particularly those in leadership positions, to see what steps they can take to reduce hostility within their immediate environments by reflecting on their reactions to provocative situations.

Novaco anger questionnaire
This questionnaire was developed by Dr Raymond W Novaco of the University of California, Irvine, and part of it is reproduced here with his permission. The objective is to determine how much anger you have.

How to use the questionnaire

The situations listed in the questionnaire below are the kind that arouse anger in us. For each of them, please rate the degree to which the incident described would anger or provoke you by using the following scale:

0	1	2	3	4
very little	little	a moderate amount	much	very much

Use the same scale for each situation. Please mark your responses by each situation. Try to imagine the incident actually happening to you, and then indicate the extent to which it would have made you angry.

In the actual situations, the degree of anger that you would experience certainly would depend on other factors that are not specified in the descriptions (such as, what kind of day you were having, exactly who was involved in the situation, how the act occurred, etc). This scale is concerned with your *general* reactions, and so the details of particular situations have been omitted. Please do your best to rate your responses in this general fashion.

The questionnaire

1. You unpack an appliance you have just bought, plug it in and discover that it doesn't work. _____
2. You are overcharged by a repairman and you have no choice but to pay him. _____
3. You are singled out for correction, when the actions of others go unnoticed. _____
4. Your car breaks down. _____
5. You are talking to someone and they don't answer you. _____
6. Someone pretends to be something they are not. _____
7. While you are struggling to carry four cups of coffee to your table in a café, someone bumps into you, spilling the coffee. _____
8. You have hung up your clothes, but someone knocks them to the floor and fails to pick them up. _____
9. You are hounded by a sales assistant from the moment that you walk into a department store. _____

10. You have made arrangements to go somewhere with a person who cancels at the last minute. _____

11. You are being joked about or teased. _____

12. Your car has stalled at a traffic light, and the driver behind you keeps blowing his horn. _____

13. You accidentally make the wrong turn in a car park. As you get out of your car someone yells at you, 'Where did you learn to drive?' _____

14. Someone makes a mistake and blames it on you. _____

15. You are trying to concentrate, but a person near you is tapping his foot. _____

16. You lend someone an important book or tool, and they fail to return it. _____

17. You have had a busy day, and the person you live with starts to complain about how you forgot to do something that you agreed to do. _____

18. You are trying to discuss something important with your partner who isn't giving you a chance to express your feelings. _____

19. You are in a discussion with someone who persists in arguing about a topic they know very little about. _____

20. Someone sticks his or her nose into an argument between you and someone else. _____

21. You need to get somewhere quickly, but the car in front of you is going 20 mph in a 30 mph zone, and you can't pass. _____

22. You step on some chewing gum. _____

23. You are being mocked by a small group of people as you pass them. _____

24. In a hurry to get somewhere, you tear a good pair of trousers by catching them on something sharp. _____

25. You use your last coin to make a phone call, but you are disconnected before you finish dialling and the coin is lost. _____

Interpreting your responses

Now that you have completed the questionnaire, you can calculate your anger level. Add up your score for each of the 25 situations and ensure that you have marked every one. You can now interpret your total score according to the following scale:

    0–45   – the amount of anger you experience is quite low, only a small percentage of the population would be as calm as you are

46–55 – you are calmer than the average person

56–75 – you respond to the irritations of daily life with the average amount of anger

76–85 – you frequently react in an angry way to life's annoyances. You are significantly more irritable than the average person. You may have been in trouble from time to time because of your impulsive, hostile outbursts. Only a small percentage of the population would be like you.

Even if you are in the top anger level, you are not a bad person. I would suggest that it is in your interest to use the techniques that I have discussed earlier to control your angry reactions.

References

P A Hauck, *Calm Down: How to Control Frustration and Anger*, Sheldon (1980)

D Burns, *Feeling Good: The New Mood Therapy*, Signet Press, New York (1981)

A Ellis, *Effective Leadership: A Rational Approach*, Institute for Rational-Emotive Therapy, New York (1972)

R W Novaco, *Anger Control: The Development and Evaluation of an Experimental Treatment*, Heath, Lexington, Massachusetts, USA (1975)

CHAPTER 8
Personal Organisation

This chapter was written originally for managers in the workplace, but the principles can be applied inside and outside the office.

How many times have you walked into someone's office and seen a disaster area: the desk covered with books and papers, a harried person answering phones as soon as they ring, stress and anxiety written all over his or her face? It's common for managers to be in this position and asking themselves 'How can I get out from underneath it all?'

Writing down goals and priorities

They key to personal organisation is planning and the writing down of goals and priorities. This should be done on a daily, weekly, monthly, yearly basis. This means every day one should write down, either at the end of the previous day, or first thing in the morning of the day in question, what you intend to do that day. This can be done on a form or a notepad – a so-called 'To Do Today' list (see page 75). As well as this, at the beginning of each week a 'Weekly Plan' list should be prepared (see page 76) and at the beginning of each month, a monthly plan list and so on, six-monthly, yearly, three-yearly. This concept of writing plans is essential to any time-management system. However, just writing down your goals is not sufficient, you must then assign some priority to them using an ABC or numerical system to identify which goals are most important to you. Once you have done that, you can then work on the most important goal first and write down the steps you will take to achieve it.

Things to do today

Date:

Task	Priority	Time needed	Done	Scheduled events
				8.00
				8.30
				9.00
				9.30
				10.00
				10.30
				11.00
				11.30
				12.00
				12.30
				1.00
				1.30
				2.00
				2.30
				3.00
				3.30
				4.00
				4.30
				5.00
Notes				5.30
				6.00
				Evening

Weekly plan

Week commencing: ....

Objectives (what I hope to achieve by the end of the week)

Activities necessary to accomplish objectives	Priority	Time needed	Which day

Important versus urgent tasks must be clearly understood because managers, in general, are subjected to the 'tyranny of the urgent'. There are a continuous demands made upon them – the average manager is interrupted once every eight minutes.

Time to plan

Managers need time to be able to carry out their planning, controlling and organising functions and they need at least one clear hour per day to think out and plan their activities. Unless they adopt certain tactics they will never get that hour. Only by writing down goals and objectives can decide what is important as opposed to what is urgent. Tasks that are considered important *and* urgent, should be done ahead of those that are deemed only urgent.

Blocking interruptions

One of the best techniques to make more effective use of your time is to block interruptions. The main interruptions to the manager are:

Telephone calls

These must be screened as far as possible. Do not answer each call yourself but arrange to have your secretary, receptionist or telephone answering service take calls wherever possible. A secretary or a receptionist can screen the calls and politely and diplomatically deal with many of those callers and refer to you the callers that only you can deal with. Alex Mackenzie's book, *The Time Trap*, has a section on the telephone that gives a clear and detailed description of how to deal with this.

Drop-in visitors

Establish a 'closed door' policy or have an 'open door' policy at fixed times during the week. See visitors by appointment. If an unexpected visitor gains entry to your office, stand up immediately, discuss the matter with that person and escort them to the door. I am not suggesting that you become anti-social and a recluse – by all means enjoy the company of your colleagues and associates at appropriate times! Socialise at morning tea, lunch or after work, but when you are trying to complete that very important report, budget or other task, then you must have blocks of uninterrupted time so that you can concentrate on the task at hand. Otherwise valuable time will be lost and it will be difficult for you to get your thoughts together in a coherent fashion if you are subjected to continual interruptions.

Mail

Many managers still open the mail themselves. Have this done by your secretary or personal assistant as far as possible and deal with it only once a day. If you do have to do it yourself, wait until the end of the day or the next morning before going through it.

Dealing with paper

This brings me to the next suggestion to assist with personal organisation, that is, how to deal with paper.

One of the key rules argued by Alan Lakein in his book *How to Get Control of Your Time and Your Life* is to handle each paper item only once. This means that you deal with letters, reports and documents when they come on to your desk once a day; deal with the letters by dictating replies if you are in a position to do so and when doing so, dictate only key ideas, your secretary or assistant can be left to compose the actual letter. Answer a letter on the original letter itself, retain a photocopy of it, and return it to the sender. This is becoming more acceptable for most internal and many external communications. Have a large wastepaper basket handy and throw out unwanted mail as soon as it arrives.

Read books like newspapers, skimming or reading only what seems to be of interest then go to the summary. Get others to read reports, articles, etc for you. Allow reading material to accumulate, take some with you when you know you will have time waiting for an appointment and use this time by skimming through some of the material.

Keep your desk as clear as possible except for what you are working on at the time and *try to complete each task before moving on to the next one.*

Dictation

Dictation is another very powerful time saving tool. You can dictate at the rate of about 150 words per minute versus a long-hand rate of five to ten words per minute. Many managers unfortunately still write in long hand.

Use dictation to reply to letters, to draft reports and to prepare other important documents. You can summarise meetings and put good ideas on tape with a small portable dictation machine when they come to mind. If your secretary seems averse to using a dictation machine, get her to try it; she will soon find that it will assist her by saving time as there will not be the necessity for face-to-face contact that regular shorthand dictation requires.

There are books available on dictating effectively as a time management tool. You can also give instructions to your colleagues on tape and report to superiors in the same way. With adequate preparation by jotting down objectives, outlines and references, you can, with practice, dictate very comprehensive and clear reports.

The manager/secretary team

Finally, I would mention the manager/secretary team. The development of this team can double the effectiveness of a manager due to the way in which the secretary can help the manager in many of the activities already mentioned above: screening telephone calls, visitors and mail, preparing papers for consideration, organising the desk, files and office layout, drafting replies to routine correspondence and providing advice to the manager. Good communication between the secretary and the manager is of vital importance as the manager can then delegate time consuming tasks to the secretary.

The objective of these suggestions is to get people to make more effective use of their time and many of these principles can be applied to the management of the home. It does not mean becoming obsessed with time management but, by scheduling your activities, you can generate time for relaxation and leisure and help clarify objectives at work and at home. This means that you will have more time for the pursuits you enjoy and value.

Twenty steps to successful time management

1. Clarify your objectives. Put them in writing. Then set out your priorities. Make sure you're getting what you really want out of life.

2. Focus on objectives, not on activities. Your most important activities are those that help you to accomplish your objectives.

3. Set yourself at least one major objective each day and achieve it.

4. Record a time log periodically to analyse how you use your time, and keep bad time habits out of your life.

5. Analyse everything you do in terms of your objectives. Find out what you do, when you do it, why you do it. Ask yourself what would happen if you didn't do it. If the answer is nothing, then stop doing it.

6. Eliminatae at least *one* time wasting activity from your life each week.

7. Plan your time. Write out a plan for each week. Ask yourself what you hope to accomplish by the end of the week and what you will need to do to achieve those results.

8. Make a list of things to do every day. Be sure it includes your daily objectives, priorities and time estimates, not just random activities.

9. Schedule your time every day to make sure you accomplish the most important things first. Be sure to leave room for the unexpected and for interruptions, but remember that things that are scheduled have a better chance of working out than things that are unscheduled.

10. Make sure that the first hour of your working day is productive.

11. Set time limits for every task you undertake.

12. Take the time to do it right the first time. You won't have to waste time doing it over again.

13. Eliminate recurring crises from your life. Find out why things keep going wrong. Learn to proact instead of react.

14. Institute a quiet hour in your day – a block of uninterrupted time for your most important tasks.

15. Develop the habit of finishing what you start. Don't jump from one

thing to another, leaving a string of unfinished tasks behind you.

16. Conquer procrastination. Learn to do it now.

17. Make better time management a daily habit. Set your objectives, clarify your priorities, plan and schedule your time. Do first things first. Resist your impulses to do unscheduled tasks. Review your activities.

18. Never spend time on *less* important things when you could be spending it on *more* important things.

19. Take time for yourself – time to dream, time to relax, time to live.

20. Develop a personal philosophy of time – what time means to you and how time relates to your life.

References

R Alex Mackenzie, *The Time Trap*, McGraw-Hill (1975)

A Lakein, *How to Get Control of Your Time and Your Life*, Gower (1985)

Time-Talk (a monthly Time Management Newsletter, published in Australia by Business Newsletter Publishers, 41 Rawson Street, Epping, NSW 2121)

J D Bates, *Dictating Effectively*, Acropolis, Washington DC, USA (1981)

M E Douglass and D N Douglass, *Manage your Time, Manage Your Work, Manage Yourself*, Amacom; distributed by Kogan Page (1980)

D N Douglass, *Choice and Compromise: A Woman's Guide To Balancing Family and Career*, Amacom; (OP) (1980)

P Drucker, *The Effective Executive*, Pan (1970)

P Drucker, *Managing in Turbulent Times*, Pan (1981)

CHAPTER 9
Coping With Change

Change is going on all the time at different rates. Change occurs at the level of our cells, making us, despite our appearance, quite different biochemically from what we were a month ago, and even more so, six months ago. At a personal level, events are occurring – we marry, have children, change jobs, change bosses, get angry, get excited, laugh, enjoy ourselves and all these events affect our brains and memories and become part of our experience which, in turn influences how we perceive future events.

In our jobs, we are working *with* others and *for* others, receiving directions, being managed and managing others, we are subjected to changes in budgets, personnel, policies that have been developed within the company in which we may or may not have any say. We experience discomfort with change when it feels out of control. Changes that are out of our control are often sudden and imposed upon us. Abrupt, sudden changes frighten us. We have trouble adapting our thinking and become confused and overwhelmed by such changes. Remember when there was a sudden change and your immediate superior was replaced, or the company decided to close down your section and you were given one week's notice, or there was an unexpected death in your family. It was the abrupt and unexpected nature of the events which played a major role in your stress reaction and generated the consequent anxiety.

Life is a process

Change is continuous but it is the *rate* of change that causes problems. Extensive research with both human beings and animals suggests that two related psychological factors can determine an individual's response to the stress of change – *controllability* and *predictability*.

Controllability is the perceived ability to escape, avoid and/or modify threatening circumstances. Predictability is the perceived ability to anticipate a particular event.

The work of Martin Seligman with animals at the University of Pennsylvania has shown that when they feel they have no control over the situation and they don't know what is going to happen, then many of them undergo what he calls 'learned helplessness'. Like animals, under these conditions people effectively give up and become unresponsive and that even if circumstances change and become better, they do not.

To increase the predictability of situations, the keyword is preparation. The more you can prepare for events, the less stressful they will be when they occur and you will be less anxious while you are awaiting the change. The fear of the unknown is a powerful stressor that needs to be reduced. The question of control is much more difficult because there are many events over which we have *no* control. However, the ability to distinguish between what we can control and what we cannot is critical. For example, it is unrealistic to attempt to change your staff's negative attitude without changing your own.

How you interact with your work environment

This is another important factor in coping with change. At one extreme, it can be a stressful, punishing interaction where you face hostility and jealousy from your colleagues, together with an unpleasant physical environment and poor conditions – let's say, a small office that is crowded, has a high turnover of staff and a hostile, threatening boss. However, it may be the only job that has come up or is likely to come up for you in the next six months, therefore, it is in your interests to learn to cope with the frustration of this job at least until you find something better.

The other extreme would be an extremely pleasant environment, exciting work, perhaps on a newspaper as a journalist, travelling with a television crew to different parts of the world and continuously being given positive feedback by the people you talk to, work with and produce for.

Most of us work in environments that are somewhere between these two extremes and which vary from time to time. However, I want to emphasise the importance of this interaction and the changes that may occur as a result of factors over which we have no control.

They might include:

- a major reorganisation due to a takeover bid;
- a new immediate boss;
- a job change, due to either relocation, retirement or redundancy;
- a change in work activity, say from sales to management, from finance to computing.

Thus techniques that will help you to tolerate frustration and stress because of changes over which you have no control are very important.

These would include, in the workplace, asking yourself such questions as 'Am I seeking a new job?', 'Am I seeking promotion?', 'Am I seeking the education and experience necessary to do my job successfully and enjoyably?', 'Am I seeking the personal skills (through courses or seminars) to communicate both at work and at home?'

How you interact with your home environment

Questions that you could ask yourself about your home life could include:

'Am I moving?', 'Am I changing my primary relationship through marriage, separation or divorce?', 'Am I changing relationships with my parents, children or other significant family members?', 'Am I changing my relationship with any of my friends or significant others such as professional colleagues?'

These questions and those relating to work are an attempt to analyse the types of change that you may have to cope with and, by doing this, you can increase the predictability and even the controllability of such changes.

How to handle change

The most important issue is to determine how you view the change, what you think about it and what techniques you can institute to manage it more effectively. I would like to draw your attention to the quotation by the Roman philosopher, Epictetus: 'Men are disturbed not by things, but by the view which they take of them.' This view is that of cognitive behavioural psychologists who argue that people need to dispute irrational thinking that occurs readily when they are confronted with change. People irrationally fear the worst, tell themselves that terrible things will happen if, say, the department is restructured and their old ways are altered. Psychologist Albert Ellis calls this 'catastrophising' and, in reality, very rarely does the worst happen.

Recently, I talked to a manager facing compulsory early retirement. His whole life had been devoted to the company for which he worked and, all of a sudden, 'they' were out to get him. He felt extremely angry with them and with the world in general and this spilt over into his personal relationships at home. I started to dispute this irrational thinking with him, arguing that nowhere was it written that he should be treated justly and fairly at all times. I suggested that it was appropriate for him to be annoyed and disappointed at what had happened, but that it was inappropriate for him to be so extremely hostile and bitter as this was now making his own life unhappy, together with that of his wife and children. I advised him to start planning and to write down future goals he would like to achieve in the light of this change. Then, rather than seeing his redundancy as a terrible catastrophe, to look at it as a challenge and to seek solutions to the problem. I suggested he list in writing the various options open to him, which he did. They included:

- A plan for seeking alternative employment;
- making use of any spare time that might arise as a result of his

redundancy to do things he had not been able to do before due to the pressure of work, such as spending more time with his children, working on a better relationship with his wife and improving the value of his home;

- exploring the possibilities of setting up his own business;
- pursuing some rewarding and pleasant activities that he had not thought of for many years.

I helped him to prepare a list of written options that he had in readiness to tackle the forthcoming change. He looked at how he was managing his time at present and how he might plan for the more effective use of his time for the future on a daily, weekly and long-term basis so that he could take the necessary steps towards attaining the new goals he had set himself.

These techniques can be applied to many of the situations described earlier when change occurs unexpectedly. By developing the sorts of skills described, you can cope with change more effectively.

Human resource management

The management of your interaction with others is a key to any change process, whether you are implementing the change or whether it is being brought about by others. How you manage to help both yourself and others in the change process will play a large role in the success or failure of your personal or work goals. You need to manage your anger, hostility and resentment to the change using the cognitive restructuring techniques that I have discussed earlier in Chapter 7, Hostility at Work. It is important to share the proposed change with those who will also be affected and to gain their support, particularly those who can help or hinder the change. In looking for support for yourself, also be aware of how you can give support to others. People do remember your 'helping hand', and they are more inclined to help if they have at least a rudimentary relationship with you. Managing people involves an *exchange* of support – otherwise, one of you begins to feel used.

If you see yourself as having difficulty dealing with people to get the kind of support you would like, take a long look at your relationship skills. There are many books and courses available to help improve your communication and assertiveness/conciliation skills.

The process of change, therefore, can be made easier by adopting suitable techniques, especially when much of the anxiety and stress is self-induced.

References

V D Lachman, *Stress Management: A Manual for Nurses*, Grune & Stratton (1983)

A Ellis and R A Harper, *A New Guide to Rational Living*, Wilshire, North Hollywood, California, USA (1975)

M J Smith, *When I Say No I Feel Guilty*, Bantam (1973)

R Bolton, *People Skills*, Prentice Hall (1980)

R E Alberti and M L Emmons, *Your Perfect Right*, Impact (1983)

M Seligman, *Helplessness*, W H Freeman (1975)

CHAPTER 10
Substance Abuse – What Can You Do?

Smoking, alcohol and drug abuse are risk factors associated with major causes of death, such as lung cancer, heart disease, accidents and suicide. This is reported in *The Health Almanac*, an American book that analyses statistics on death and disease. Obesity is another major problem in advanced industrialised societies.

Smoking is still a common habit and causes relatively minor disturbance to the person who smokes or his close associates until cancer or emphysema appears. Alcohol and heroin, however, are different as, once a person is addicted a great deal of self-defeating behaviour and damage to others can result – jobs can be lost, violence and criminal activity often occur, gaol may follow, all to meet the demands of the habit.

Over-eating is a widespread problem, leading to obesity and an increased risk of developing hypertension and diabetes, together with negative feelings and attitudes because overweight people do not like their appearance.

Theories of addiction

Theories of addiction are plentiful. There are suggestions that it is genetic and a disease state (alcholism is called Jellenick's disease by some people) or that an addiction is a conditioned habit that a person has learned. The relief and the good feelings that quickly follow the taking of these substances provides the incentive to carry on taking them.

Pharmacologists and neuroscientists have found different receptors in the brain to which drugs attach themselves; in the case of morphine they are called opiate receptors. Addicting drugs are thought to bind to these structures in the brain and cause chemical changes in the nerve cells. These changes produce the addiction. Thus methadone binds to the heroin receptors and this signals to the brain that they have been satisfied and the craving for the drug ceases. Neurochemical research has only just begun to look into these questions and there are still many unknowns and contradictions – why do some people and not others become addicted and why can some people stop easily and others cannot?

For many reasons, people want to stop taking substances that are causing them to downgrade themselves and behave badly with their families and colleagues. We all know people who have problems at work or at home with one of these substances or we may have one ourselves. In my work I am often asked 'How can I stop drinking?', 'How can I stop smoking?', 'How can I stop eating unnecessarily?', 'How can I stop my need for a fix every day?'

Reasons given by people for using drugs

Escape from reality
Getting high is the perfect escape from ... (depression, anxiety, boredom, anger).
Once I'm high, I don't have to deal with anything bad.

Dealing with hopelessness
There's nothing else for me.
There's nothing else to make me feel good.
I'm a born loser anyhow.
If I didn't get high, I might attempt suicide.
I have no future, so I might as well feel good now.

Replacing social skills
I can deal with people better when I'm using ...
If I'm straight I'll feel tense, inferior, awkward.
I won't know what to say.
I'm more outgoing when I'm high, I joke more.

Escape from stressful individuals or situations
I won't have to deal with my ... (parents, wife, girlfriend).
I'll be able to face the job better.'
The arguing, shouting (the lack of money) won't bother me.

Group membership
It makes me feel as though I belong to something.
My friends would reject me if I didn't use it.
They'd think I was weak if I refused.
It makes me feel like a man.
It keeps me from worrying about being attractive enough.

Psychotherapy

I believe a sound approach to treating drug abuse is based on a therapeutic relationship between the person seeking help and someone else, usually a professional. The therapist shows the person techniques that can be used to manage the craving for the substance and provide a different way of thinking about himself, together with the necessary monitoring of a programme that has been set up by mutual agreement, usually by means of a series of meetings during which progress, thinking and behaviour change is discussed and reviewed.

Alcoholics Anonymous is a form of group therapy in which people who have overcome alcohol addiction show other people how to do it by a set of rules. Members explain their problems and provide a social support system for those who are participating. Unfortunately, many people withdraw and relapse but, nevertheless, it is an approach that has widespread acceptance in the community. It is cost-effective because it is non-residential with minimal overheads and meetings occuring all over the country every night of the week.

Cognitive/behaviour therapy

When clients seek my help, I use a cognitive/behavioural approach and, once the decision to give up the habit has been made, I will then work on the person's thinking about *why* he needs to take the drug and the *benefits* of doing without it. There are a number of areas on which I concentrate, these include:

- helping him or her to overcome feelings of hopelessness and low self-esteem;
- anxiety because of interpersonal relationships and performance problems at work;
- often social skills need to be developed, together with assertive as opposed to passive or aggressive behaviour;
- ways of dealing with anger.

Techniques to help the person refuse the problem substance (alcohol, heroin, desserts/cakes, cigarettes) are explained; this means using coping mechanisms other than the substance itself. They include relaxation and distraction techniques. For example, if a person in the past took the substance when he was bored, he is taught to devise a list of activities that will distract him and, in effect, would take the place of the substance. Often a person takes the substance because he has become too tired, too tense, too anxious or too depressed. If he is tense, he will be taught to engage in some physical activity; if he is tired he should sleep; if he is depressed he can use the techniques of Professor A T Beck, which include disputing and challenging the cognitive triad associated with depression – a negative view of oneself, the world and the future. Professor Beck in his book, *Cognitive Therapy of Depression*, outlines these techniques very effectively. They dispute and challenge the irrational thoughts when they arise often automatically. I have discussed this more fully in Chapter 3, Coping With Depression.

Behaviour therapy methods are also used. People write down their negative perceptions and thoughts and then answer them in rational fashion on a special form (see Daily Record of Dysfunctional Thoughts Form, pages 30–33, and below).

Self-statement record

It has been found that negative beliefs and self-defeating private monologues are common obstacles to controlling drug use. The purpose of treatment is to make you aware of these negative thoughts and of ways in which you can alter them; to chart these negative statements, which appear when you take the problem substance, or start to take it.

How to fill in your self-statement record

1. In the *'Self-defeating self-statement'* column, write one or two of these statements if they are present. If the self-statements are not self-defeating or not present, write 'none'.
2. *'Category'* (C) column. There are four categories of negative self-statements. Use the first letter of whichever word most nearly coincides with your own self-statements – Capabilities, Excuses, Specific Substances, and Self-Blame.
3. In the *'Degree of belief'* (DB) column record any number on a scale from 0 to 5 your degree of belief. 0 for no belief at all to 5 for complete belief.
4. In the *'Counter self-statement'* column, place the thoughts that challenged the self-defeating one. If you did not put anything in this column, write 'none'.
5. In the next column, *'Degree of belief'* (DB) write the degree of belief, from 0 to 5, you had for this counter thought.
6. Record the drugs or substances encountered.
7. In the last column write whether you took drugs or not.

A variety of behaviour therapy techniques are available to encourage physical activity in the case of tension. Imagery and relaxation are also useful here and can be helpful in inducing sleep. Rewards and penalties that are agreed between the client and the therapist can be very useful too. For instance, if the person agrees not to have a cigarette, a drink or a fix for the next three days, then he will give himself some special treat: a film, a concert or something that he particularly enjoys. However, if he does indulge an agreed penalty will apply; he will do something that he dislikes, such as talking to someone he finds boring or making out a cheque to some cause or political party that he abhors, to be sent by the therapist. A wide variety of contracts are possible here.

Challenge your thinking

Another important method is to get the person to challenge his

Example of a completed self-statement record

Date	Self-defeating self-statement 1	C 2	DB 3	Counter self-statement 4	DB 5	Drug taking 6	Yes or No 7
4/2	A beer would be really good right now.	S	5	You're trying to feel better instead of getting better.	4	Alcohol/beer	No
8/2	I'm just naturally weak.	C	5	It is difficult to change habits but difficult doesn't mean impossible. I wasn't born weak.	2	Alcohol/2 bottles of wine	Yes
10/2	What's the use of trying when I know I'll fail again.	B	4	How do I know how I'll feel if I don't try? There's a first time for everything, including success.	5	Large helping of dessert	No

thinking and his taking of the substance. There is a close connection between the two and it is important to break the cycle. A technique called referenting is useful. This involves having a person learn to replace the meaning that he habitually assigns to stimulus words with a wider range of more objective meanings. As an example of referenting, adverse as well as pleasant and neutral meanings of such words as 'heroin', 'clean', and 'alcohol' are brought to mind. You can control feelings of compulsion, as when you think you *have* to smoke or over-eat by vigorously disputing that 'have to' and making it such a strong thought that you can inhibit your desire.

Joseph Danysh, in his book *Stop Without Quitting*, shows how you can change your desire to smoke by forcing yourself, many times, to bring to mind all the major meanings of 'smoking' and 'quitting'. Thus you can make 'smoking' mean to you 'ease', 'sophistication', 'relaxation' and 'enjoyment' and fail to keep thinking about the 'pain', 'expense', 'sickness' and 'death' that it

Date	Self-defeating self-statement 1	C 2	DB 3	Counter self-statement 4	DB 5	Drug taking 6	Yes or No 7

also really means. If you constantly bring to your mind the whole range of meanings, you will look at smoking very differently and come to feel differently about it.

Relapsing

A common problem with substance-dependent people is that, after they resolve never to indulge again, they will, almost invariably, find themselves in some situation where circumstances are so overpowering that they will take the substance. The danger in this situation arises, not so much in their taking of the substance, but in their saying to themselves 'I've blown it. I might as well go on and take some more.' The therapist's task is to try to help the person learn *not* to think in this way. Once they have broken their restraint, they are instructed to redouble their efforts to control their behaviour instead of thinking, 'I've wrecked things completely, I might as well go the whole way.'

The idea substance dependent people have that they lose all restraint after the first drink, the first slice of cake, the first puff on a cigarette, the first shot of heroin, is often a cognitive distortion. Invariably there will have been past occasions when, after having only one taste of a substance they did not go on indulging themselves. Thus, by using challenging self-talk, this type of self-fulfilling prophecy can be changed.

Donald Meichenbaum, in his book *Cognitive Behaviour Modification*, suggests ways in which a person may become aware of the change in his thinking. Whenever you find yourself losing control over your urge to take the problem substance, pay attention to what you are saying to yourself, start looking for those sentences and thoughts. Think of questions and challenges to what you are saying. For example, in answer to 'A couple of drinks would really be good right now', the rational 'You are trying to feel better instead of getting better.' To 'I really need some smack' answer, 'There is a lot of difference between *wanting* something and *needing* it.'

I am not suggesting that this is easy; it isn't, and it will cause discomfort and pain at times, but there is no reason why you should not have to endure some difficulty and unpleasantness in life in order to achieve a desirable goal. It is not terrible to be deprived of what you momentarily want, just frustrating, and the goal will be worth it.

Coping statements
The following are some general counters that can be used in a variety of situations:

- 'Avoiding short-term difficulty is tempting, but I had better consider both long- and short-term consequences.'
- 'If it is worth doing (changing habits) it's worth doing poorly or slowly. Progress may be one step backwards for every two steps forward, but it's still progress.'
- 'No matter how hard I try I'll never be perfect, but perfection is not my goal.'
- 'If I fail it doesn't make *me* a failure; it makes me a person who has failed this time but who can succeed the next time, or the time after that.'
- 'Believing that a habit I learned in the past is unchangeable is a cop-out and a substitute for reality. In reality, habits are changeable.'
- 'There is no magical way my habits are going to change themselves.'
- 'Where is my evidence?' 'Show me the facts!' 'Is there any proof?'
- 'People are generally very slow to learn new ways of thinking and behaving, but *slow* does not mean *impossible*; it just requires patience, which means tolerating frustration.'

The last response – 'tolerating frustration' – is a very important one because that is a critical skill to develop, to overcome a low frustration threshold. I have discussed this in Chapter 5, Frustration – Make it Work for You.

These cognitive techniques and debates with yourself are very important because they help to change the thinking and belief system of the person using them. This new thinking will change his feelings about the *absolute necessity* for the substance to one of *desire*, with the realisation that he can survive in the immediate future without it.

The importance of working with a therapist is that the therapist can monitor the addicted person's behaviour. If there are relapses, these can be dealt with by discussion in a therapeutic environment without the recrimination, blame, self-criticism and depression that usually accompanies such relapses.

Challenging your negative thoughts

Cravings

I really need some smack.	There is a lot of difference between wanting something and needing it.
A beer would really be good right now.	You're trying to feel better instead of getting better.
That cake will help my morale.	It will lower your morale by making you lose control.

Self-blame

What in the hell is wrong with me? Why can't I change?	No one is perfect, and it is big-headed to think I should never make mistakes.
There is something wrong with me for not being able to control my use of drugs.	My drug-taking behaviour is a fraction of my total self. It is an over-generalisation to rate myself on this.
I shouldn't have taken that.	Blaming myself doesn't help me to change my habits and it may do more harm than good.

Capabilities

I just don't have the willpower.	I have changed other habits and have controlled my drug use before.
I'm just naturally weak.	It is difficult to change habits, but difficult does not mean impossible. I was not *born* weak.
This will never work for me.	Where is the evidence that I can't do this?
I'm too discouraged now to try to resist temptation.	This is frustrating, but in the long run it will be worth it. I may as well start now as later. Then I'll be ahead.

Excuses

I can't control myself when I am at a party	It is more difficult under these circumstances, but not impossible. I welcome a test of my ability.
My friends made me do it.	No one can really make me do anything unless they are holding a gun at my head.
I can't go without drugs when I'm down.	I just have to remember what my main goal is and not be taken in by these side issues.
What's the use of trying when I know I'll fail again?	How do I know I'll fail if I don't try? There's a first time for everything, including success.

Group therapy is a very useful method for helping people to deal with their addictions because it is cost-effective and participants derive support from the interaction with others who have similar problems. They can also help one another through difficult periods and monitor and look at the changes and progress in an atmosphere that is stimulating, provocative and often very enjoyable.

We can all be therapeutic to colleagues, friends and family who have drug abuse problems and be mindful of the principle of parity – that people are not worth any less because of their self-defeating behaviour but must be accepted as human beings who have the potential to help themselves.

References

A T Beck, A J Rush, B F Shaw and G Emery, *Cognitive Therapy of Depression*, Guildford, New York (1979)

A T Beck and G Emery, *Cognitive Therapy of Substance Abuse*, Center for Cognitive Therapy, Philadelphia, Pennsylvania (1977)

D Burns, *Feeling Good; The New Mood Therapy*, Signet Books, New American Library, New York (1980)

A Ellis, *Reason and Emotion in Psychotherapy*, Lyle Stuart, New York (1962)

A Ellis and R A Harper, *A New Guide to Rational Living*, Prentice-Hall, Englewood Cliffs, New Jersey, USA (1975)

A Fay, *The Invisible Diet*, Manor, New York (1980)

J Haley, *Strategies of Psychotherapy*, Grune & Stratton, New York (1963)

G Kelly, *The Psychology of Personal Constructs* (Volumes I and II), Norton, New York (1955)

A D Kidman, 'Neurochemical and Cognitive Aspects of Depression', *Progress in Neurobiology*, Vol 24, pp 187–197 (1985).

A A Lazarus, *In the Mind's Eye*, Rawson, New York (1977)

P Lewinsohn, R F Munoz, M A Youngren, A M Zeiss, *Control Your Depression*, Prentice Hall, Englewood Cliffs, New Jersey, USA (1978)

T A Madden, I R Turner and E J Eckenfels, *The Health Almanac*, Rawson, New York (1982)

D Meichenbaum, *Cognitive Behaviour Modification*, Plenum Press, New York (1977)

R B Stuart, *Act Thin, Stay Thin*, Mayflower/Granada (1982)

CHAPTER 11
Stress and the Individual

If the twentieth century is to be known as the age of science and technology, it also will be known as the age of stress and anxiety. Certainly the awareness of stress is increasing and this is shown by the spate of articles, books and relaxation classes that are being offered on this subject.

The current concepts of stress have developed from the ideas of Hans Selye who started work on this subject in the 1930s and continued until his death at the age of 75 in 1982. Selye defined stress, or, more correctly, the stress response, as the non-specific response of the body to any demand made upon it. Selye showed that a wide variety of external stimuli will produce a release of certain chemicals in the brain.

The stress response

Walter Cannon from Harvard, earlier in the century, was the first to describe the role of chemicals in the 'fight or flight' reaction, but it was Selye who unified and promoted this stress concept. The agents or stimuli that produce the stress response in the body are called 'stressors' and the interaction can be shown in the following equation.

Stressors + Individual Make-up = Stress Response

Stress responses are necessary for the day-to-day adaptability of human beings to their environment and result in the maintenance of an internal steady state (homeostasis). Thus we all need a certain level of stress response in order to live and to achieve our goals.

If there is too *little* stress, which happens when we are bored, or too *much* external stimulation, the stress response is unfavourable and has the potential to make people ill. Then it is labelled 'distress'. The constant anxiety and worry in a susceptible person may lead to hypertension, ulcers or muscle pain. If the stress response is favourable and results in improvement in physical or mental functioning, it is called 'eustress'. An example of this would be vigorous exercise which can improve the functioning of the heart and lungs and result in a decreased chance of heart attack.

Types of stressors
External stressors can be subdivided into three groups:

1. **Physical stressors**
   These include such things as chemicals, drugs, extremes of temperature, exercise, infectious microbes, trauma.
2. **Social stressors**
   These are also known as life changing events and result from the interaction of the individual with his environment. They include the death of a loved one, loss of a job, retirement, divorce, financial reversal. Pleasant events, however, such as engagement announcements, marriage ceremonies, financial windfalls, promotions, can also be social stressors.
3. **Psychological stressors**
   These, because of their recurrent nature, are often the most damaging kind and may be brought on by physical or social stressors, or may often be self-induced. Psychological stressors include intense emotions such as frustration, anxiety, fear, guilt, anger and feelings of inferiority and low self worth.

The individual make-up of the person is critical in determining the duration and the intensity of the stress response. This includes that person's genes and such things as age, experience, health, physical fitness and, most importantly, the way in which he or she deals with perceptions of events.

There is a whole range of diseases that are thought to be stress related and I will briefly mention some of these. They are cardiovascular disease, depression, muscle-related conditions, such as tension headaches, backaches, ulcers, and certain allergic diseases, such as chronic urticaria (hives) and hayfever, to name but a few. Alcoholism, obesity and drug addiction are also often related to stressful situations.

Different people will react differently to a given set of stressors. A young person facing public speaking for the first time may find that he feels extremely anxious, causing a very marked stress response, whereas an experienced politician would endure practically no stress response facing the same audience.

Coping mechanisms

The anxieties and frustrations of modern urban living are often the cause of excessive stress responses in a large number of people. This is due to irrational beliefs and expectations that many people have about themselves, their work or their families.

The coping mechanisms they use to deal with stress are many and varied and range from drinking and smoking to watching television, gardening and avoidance behaviour to alleviate the tension that people may feel in particular situations. Regular aerobic exercise is a well established coping mechanism that many people use to relieve stress and the burgeoning of fitness clubs, jogging, aerobic dancing classes, and so on is evidence of this. Exercise is an appropriate means for reducing the stress response because you feel relaxed after the vigorous aerobic exercise. Walking for 45 minutes at a time is an excellent aerobic exercise for almost all ages. I recommend Ken Cooper's book, *New Aerobics* for its comprehensive range of exercise plans.

In my experience as a consultant to industry and in dealing with individuals suffering from stress-induced anxiety and depression there are two very good ways of coping with stress.

Muscle relaxation

The first is muscle relaxation, combined with visual imagery. This technique, originally described by Jacobsen and more recently by Herbert Benson in his book *The Relaxation Response*, has been shown to be effective in reducing such things as high blood pressure, anxiety, muscle pain and insomnia. However, the work of Professor Arnold Lazarus has shown how very important visual imagery can be in helping to reduce excessive, undesirable stress responses. The key elements in producing the relaxation response are:

- a passive attitude;
- a quiet environment;
- a technique for relaxing muscles while concentrating on a particular word;
- pleasant, satisfying mental images (this can be done on a daily basis for 10 to 20 minutes and improvement occurs with practice).

Rational-emotive therapy

The second method is a psychological one using a cognitive behavioural approach and specifically the Rational-Emotive Therapy (RET) techniques described by Albert Ellis and his colleagues in New York.

The theory argues that your perceptions of events that are going on around you determine your emotional and behavioural responses. Thus, negative feelings, can be altered by changing the beliefs or thinking of the individual. Anxiety and hostility at work can then be altered if your so-called irrational ideas about succeeding perfectly at everything you do, or wanting to be treated with complete and utter fairness and justice at all times by your superiors, can be challenged and altered. Then, many of the inappropriate negative feelings can be reduced to more appropriate ones, for example hostility and anger to annoyance, depression to sadness, resentment to disappointment. According to this theory, therefore, it is important for people not to devalue themselves or others on the basis of certain behaviour patterns, such as lying, getting drunk, abusive language, but rather to accept that people will behave badly at times, some much more frequently than others, but not let this behaviour and the perceptions and subsequent feelings aroused become powerful, negative stressors.

The cognitive behavioural approach to dealing with psychological stressors is probably one of the most useful methods available to overcome these common problems, I have discussed this more fully in Chapter 2, Tactics for Change.

Illness and lifestyle

The heaviest burdens of illness in western industrialised societies are related to aspects of individual behaviour, especially long-term patterns of behaviour that we often refer to as 'lifestyle'.

Lifestyle factors include diet, activity or exercise, ability to relax, ability to relate effectively with others. A high percentage of deaths from the main mortality factors can be traced to lifestyle. For example, those who are able to modify their diets and control their consumption of alcohol, cigarettes, food and drugs, will be less at risk of early death.

If people will consider trying the cognitive behavioural techniques mentioned to calm themselves in an increasingly demanding environment, to face anxious and hostile situations and to change their inappropriate emotional responses, they will, in most cases, have better relationships with their peers and families. They will be perceived as appropriate models for others to imitate. Thus, they can help to reduce the amount of unnecessary stress and anxiety for themselves and those around them.

References

H Selye, *Stress Without Distress*, Corgi (1987)

D R Morse and M L Furst, *Stress for Success*, Van Nostrand Reinhold (1982)

H Benson and M Klipper, *The Relaxation Response*, Collins, Fount Paperbacks (1977)

H Benson and R L Allen, 'How Much Stress is too Much?', *Harvard Business Review*, pages 86–92 (September/October, 1980)

C L Cooper and R Payne (Editors), *Stress at Work*, John Wiley (1978)

H Benson, 'Systemic Hypertension and the Relaxation Response', *New England Journal of Medicine*, Vol 296, pages 1152–5 (1977)

A Ellis and R A Harper, *A New Guide to Rational Living*, Wilshire, North Hollywood, California, USA (1975)

K H Cooper *New Aerobics*, Bantam, New York (1970)

N B Belloc, 'Relationship of Health Practices and Mortality', *Preventative Medicine*, Vol 2, pages 67–81 (1973)

J Madders, *Stress and Relaxation*, Martin Dunitz (1979)

R Montgomery, *Coping with Stress*, Pitman, Sydney, Australia (1982)

A Ellis, *Effective Leadership*, Institute for Rational-Emotive Therapy, New York (1972)

S Cotler and J Guerra, *Assertion Training*, Research Press, Champaign, Illinois, USA (1976)

H Weiner, *Total Swimming*, Simon & Schuster, New York (1980)

A D Kidman, 'Stress Cognition and the Nervous System', *Neurochemistry International*, Vol 6, No 6, pages 715–20 (1984)

RET Self-Help Form

(A) ACTIVATING EVENTS: thoughts, or feelings that happened just before I felt emotionally disturbed or acted self-defeatingly: _____

_____

(B) BELIEFS – IRRATIONAL BELIEFS (IBs) leading to my CONSEQUENCE (emotional disturbance or self-defeating behaviour). Circle all that apply to these ACTIVATING EVENTS **(A)**.	**(D) DISPUTES** for each circled IRRATIONAL BELIEF. Examples: *'Why* MUST I do very well?' *'Where is it written* that I am a BAD PERSON?' *'Where is the evidence* that I MUST be approved or accepted?'
1. I MUST do well or very well!	
2. I am a BAD OR WORTHLESS PERSON when I act weakly or stupidly.	
3. I MUST be approved or accepted by people I find important!	
4. I am a BAD UNLOVABLE PERSON if I get rejected.	
5. People MUST treat me fairly and give me what I NEED!	
6. People who act immorally are undeserving, ROTTEN PEOPLE!	
7. People MUST live up to my expectations or it is TERRIBLE!	
8. My life MUST have few major hassles or troubles.	
9. I CAN'T STAND really bad things or very difficult people!	
10. It's AWFUL or HORRIBLE when major things don't go my way!	
11. I CAN'T STAND IT when life is really unfair!	
12. I NEED to be loved by someone who matters to me a lot!	

(C) CONSEQUENCE or CONDITION: disturbed feeling or self-defeating behaviour
that I produced and would like to change: _____

_____

(E) EFFECTIVE RATIONAL BELIEFS (RBs) to
replace my IRRATIONAL BELIEFS (IBs).
Examples: *'I'd PREFER to do very well but I don't HAVE
TO.' 'I am a PERSON WHO acted badly, not a BAD
PERSON.' 'There is no evidence that I HAVE TO be
approved, though I would LIKE to be.'*

....
....
....
....
....
....
....
....
....
....
....
....
....
....
....
....
....
....
....
....
....
....
....
....
....
....
....
....
....
....

(B) BELIEFS – IRRATIONAL BELIEFS (IBs) leading to my CONSEQUENCE (emotional disturbance or self-defeating behaviour). Circle all that apply to these ACTIVATING EVENTS (A).	(D) DISPUTES for each circled IRRATIONAL BELIEF. Examples: 'Why MUST I do very well?' 'Where is it written that I am a BAD PERSON?' 'Where is the evidence that I MUST be approved or accepted?'
13. I NEED a good deal of immediate gratification and HAVE TO feel miserable when I don't get it!	
Additional irrational beliefs:	
14.	
15.	
16.	
17.	
18.	

(F) FEELINGS and BEHAVIOUR PATTERNS I experienced after arriving at my EFFECTIVE RATIONAL BELIEFS: _____

....
....
....
....
....
....
....
....
....
....
....
....
....
....
....
....
....
....
....
....
....
....
....
....
....
....
....
....
....
....
....
....
....

I will work hard to repeat my effective rational beliefs forcefully to myself on many occasions so that I can make myself less disturbed now and act less self-defeatingly in the future.

Rational responses for you
to cut out and keep with you
or put on your bulletin board

I don't like frustration

but I can stand it.

Life is a hassle. *Tough.*
Where is it written that it
should be easy?

Because I or others behave
badly does not mean
we are bad people.

Demands are not healthy
for me. It is in my
interest to change demands
into strong preferences.

Further Reading from Kogan Page

Assert Yourself: How to Do a Good Deal Better with Others
A Practical Guide to Effective Listening
Speak With Confidence
Study Skills Strategies: How to Learn More in Less Time
Successful Self-Management: A Sound Approach to Personal Effectiveness

Better Management Skills Series

Effective Meeting Skills
Effective Performance Appraisals
Effective Presentation Skills
The Fifty-Minute Supervisor
How to Communicate Effectively
How to Develop a Positive Attitude
How to Motivate People
Make Every Minute Count
Successful Negotiation
Team Building